SHINGLE

and

STONE

shingle and stone

THOMAS

houses

KLIGERMAN

thomas a. kligerman
written with mitchell owens

CONTENTS

PREFACE

A book is a mirror.

It is a chance to pause and look back at my work as if it were done by someone else—or others—as it is also a reminder that architecture is not a solitary pursuit.

From my first studio classes in architecture, guided by my professors or helped along by my fellow students, designing buildings has been, to a greater or lesser degree, a collective effort. That is not to say that I have relinquished the lead, but it would not be true if I said everything I ever did was created by me alone. The vision in this book is one of a slow and patient search and experimentation, taking its cues and inspiration from many sources, delving into the thousands of books on the shelves of the office library, and recalling memories of travel across the globe.

The evolution of this work was always a conversation. Beginning under Robert A. M. Stern at Columbia College and then later with other professors at the Yale School of Architecture, followed by working in Stern's office, and culminating in my thirty-year collaboration with my partners, John Ike and Joel Barkley. John, Joel, and I learned together, cajoling, critiquing, challenging one another. Even while working on our individual projects under the umbrella of Ike Kligerman Barkley, each of us influenced the others. Our styles differed, but the truth is that each of us had an effect on the others. We borrowed ideas from one another to develop the firm's work. I often wove ideas of theirs into my projects, sometimes openly and sometimes surreptitiously, giving them my own spin. And it was often a surprise—and always an honor—to see their interpretations of something I had done appear in their houses.

For the last few years, I have spent time thinking about American architecture and trying to develop a more focused point of view about design. Equally, John and Joel have started to pursue personal interests: John's fascination with midcentury design, his passion for the California coast, while still giving shingle style classics his own twist, his deep skill at interior design and incorporating local artisans' work into his projects. And Joel, the gentleman architect and gardener supreme, perhaps preferring the solitude of his woodland aerie, is exploring designs for residential architecture through beautiful watercolors and drawings resulting in houses of exquisite detail and form.

As we all grew together and separately, collaboratively and individually, it was natural for us to each want to set up solo practices. And we are doing so: John on the West Coast, Joel in New Jersey, and I at Kligerman Architecture + Design in New York. We each look to the future with great excitement, to our continuing friendship and respect for each other. This book of my work is a look in the mirror, laying the foundation for the future with my new partners Joseph Carline, Drew Davis, Margie Lavender, and Ross Padluck as well as principal and director of design Alex Eng. It is a journey I look forward to undertaking as we help our clients realize their dreams.

AMERICAN INSPIRATION

When I graduated from the Yale School of Architecture in the 1980s, I knew exactly what I wanted to do professionally: I wanted to be an American architect designing American architecture. But what exactly did that mean? The search for an answer has been my quest of the past forty years, through study, travel, sketching, listening to clients, learning from colleagues, putting in the 10,000 hours required to develop an almost unconscious skill for the craft of designing and

OPPOSITE: *A taut shingled skin wraps the gables, chimneys, and roof of our house in East Hampton, New York.* ABOVE: *A late nineteenth-century house on a bluff in Rhode Island incorporates the gables and porches that define the shingle style.*

building so that your mind can investigate larger concepts of form and history. I was fortunate, as a young man, to know what I didn't know, which led me to constantly seek a deeper understanding of my chosen métier. I still yearn for deeper knowledge, always, to explore the possibilities, to lay a foundation on the shoulders of giants guiding me to my own expression as an American architect.

The history of American buildings, of American taste, has been influenced by so many other cultures, brought here by the seekers of a new home in a place free from the conventions and strictures of their roots. Yet they carried the memories of their origins and sought to reinvent these forms to shelter themselves with something familiar and comfortable but adapted to their new life and hopes. And as the young country prospered, expanded, and flourished, the possibilities for what they could build for themselves expanded as well.

Stately and well-mannered Georgian architecture crossed the Atlantic Ocean from eighteenth-century England; mansard-roofed mansions of nineteenth-century Paris defined the grand houses of millionaires from Manhattan to San Francisco. The French Norman vocabulary, from picturesque *manoirs* to noble *châteaux*, had an enormous impact on the aspirational plutocrats of the early twentieth century while the Gothic vocabulary found a home everywhere from the Hudson Valley to college and university campuses

TOP: *The "Gray Ladies" of Weekapaug, Rhode Island, look out over the Atlantic Ocean.* **ABOVE**: *Gables and dormers catch the setting sun on a summer evening.* **OPPOSITE**: *Isaac Bell house, McKim, Mead & White, 1881–83, Newport, Rhode Island.*

across the country. From the large metropolis to the small town, Americans housed their cultural institutions in Beaux-Arts grandeur. All these influences and more have trickled down into the melting pot that is American taste—and, to be honest, I love them. They have inspired me to reinvent, again, to be inspired by the vocabularies of the past, yet reshaped and reconfigured to express my own language of form. For years, they have had an unmistakable impact on the architecture that our studio has created. But can any of those expressions really be described as American?

Since 2008 or so, I have been casting my mind back to the architecture around which I grew up in New England, particularly the summer cottages of the Rhode Island coastline. Whatever shape they took, from sugar-cube simple to grand, asymmetrical informality, they were covered in cedar shingles. Conjured by innovative architects such as Stanford White, William Ralph Emerson, and Bruce Price, those early shingle style houses always had something elemental in their character: grounded and humble, yet also inventive in silhouette and detail. Logical courses of shingles suddenly could become flights of fancy and pattern, in the manner of classic American patchwork quilts, one basic material shaped and combined into lively patterns that could be complicated in composition yet always felt relaxed. Small wonder that Vincent Scully, the brilliant Yale architectural historian, not only coined the catchy term "shingle style"—known as "modern colonial" by its early practitioners—but also codified that architectural genre in his influential book *The Shingle Style and the Stick Style* (1955).

Scully followed that book in 1989 with a related volume that put the shingle style into an emotional context, a book that was evocatively entitled *The Architecture of the American Summer*. As he explained, and as I understood from my earliest years, shingle style houses in the last quarter of the nineteenth century were constructed for seasonal enjoyment. They punctuated seaside resorts, they were perched on cliffs, and they were tucked into wooded landscapes. Shingle style buildings had a three-dimensional escapist quality, yet however inventive they were aesthetically, they always came across as simple and unpretentious, wrapped with porches for lounging and distinguished with towers for viewing. At their best, shingle style houses are the architectural equivalent of a soulmate: comforting, dependable, and emotionally supportive. I loved the way they looked, the way they smelled, whether rain-soaked or sun-dried, and the way they sounded. Sound is a sense that nobody discusses in architecture, but it is crucial, and often the most viscerally remembered: the proverbial American screen door slamming shut, shutters rattling in the night breeze, footsteps racing up the back stairs. These were the buildings of my childhood, and I have carried them in my mind and my heart ever since. They have had a tremendous influence on me and my work, and I have taken a great deal of pleasure in researching them and in visiting my favorites, among them Stanford White's inspiring house for Isaac Bell in Newport.

When I was fourteen, my family moved to New Mexico from the East Coast, trading coastal ponds, rolling farmland, and beach dunes covered in silvery green reeds for the Sangre de Cristo mountains, a sunbaked desert of sand and stone, blinding light, and hills dotted in piñon pines. The American Southwest was a world that was the exact opposite of where I had spent my formative years, and it shook me to the core. Not only was the landscape so utterly different, so were the buildings. Instead of wood houses with walls that were mere inches thick, the adobe buildings had walls that could be up to six feet thick, a few even more. It was an architecture of stacked stone and mud bricks; you can sense the exertion and stamina it took to create those massive, rounded forms. They seemed to emerge directly from the earth rather than being built on top of it. Their forms were solid, their edges were soft, and their presence had a monumental quality.

New Mexico's built landscape also introduced my eyes to something new: the ways sunlight and shadow react differently depending on a building's silhouette, its materials, and landscape around it. Sunlight in the American desert is strong,

even relentless, with few natural interruptions across the desert mesas and canyons. Sunlight on the East Coast is more multidimensional, especially at the seashore, where it is reflected by the ocean, softened by dunes, and diffused by the moist air. That lesson is one that I have carried with me throughout my career, especially as I explore the sculptural possibilities that a house offers. Thanks to sunlight, something as seemingly insignificant as the depth of a window can become a powerful element in the dimensionality of a building, as shadows are cast, lengthening throughout the day until they disappear altogether, only to begin again the next morning. It is a form of alchemy, of magic.

Even more impressive to me than the work of New Mexico's early twentieth-century architects, such as John Gaw Meem, the maestro of Santa Fe, were the buildings that had inspired them. Not only Spanish colonial structures but more importantly the eons-old settlements created by and for the builders of the pueblos, notably in Taos. This is an architectural expression that stretches back into prehistory—dense and stately and impassive, stoic in form and thick in construction. Indigenous cultures had been creating those massed dwellings for thousands of years, and I was mesmerized by the ruins of pueblos in Chaco Canyon and the cliff dwellings in Mesa Verde, from the immensity of the walls to the structural engineering to the broad-shouldered forms that seemed sculpted rather than built.

Years later, during my residency at the American Academy in Rome, I was reminded of that density when I began to explore ancient Roman buildings. They had a similar scale and monumentality as the New Mexican buildings of my youth, a familiar language of deep-cut openings and immense shadows. More lessons were impressed on me on solitary walks through the city, where, sketchbook in hand, I found myself exploring that sun-and-shadow alchemy as it animated the Colosseum and deepened the beauty of Renaissance palazzi, making magic as it interacted with carved stone, stacked bricks, and terra-cotta tiles.

TOP: *San Francisco de Asís Mission Church, Ranchos de Taos, New Mexico.* **ABOVE**: *Pueblo Bonito, Chaco Canyon, New Mexico.* **OPPOSITE**: *The entrance porch to our Water Mill house.*

You cannot learn about that in a class; you have to experience it on your own, taking your time and literally watching time pass and its effect on what you are seeing.

That kind of experience sparks new ideas. That is why so many of us look back at architects who reshaped and reinterpreted the norms. For all my interest in American architecture, in identifying what that is, perhaps ironically, I take an enormous amount of inspiration from people such as Sir John Soane and Sir Edwin Lutyens, British architects who worked within a vocabulary—namely classicism—and taught it new things, unconventional things.

I can only imagine what their more hidebound contemporaries must have thought when they saw those two men, working a century apart from one another, exploring what was possible.

They made architecture sing. Add to them the work of the mannerist Giulio Romano, the Gothic revivalist Augustus Pugin, and the arts and crafts genius C. F. A. Voysey, among other talents that I admire. The reason architects refer to them today is not because they did the right thing, the correct thing; it is because they dared to experiment and convinced clients to take that journey with them.

Their work may be the reason why I have been experimenting so much in recent years. When I am presented with a shingle style commission, I find myself searching for ways to subvert it, to give it renewed freshness, to do something unexpected—and most of all, to create something interesting.

I count myself fortunate to have been educated by some of the best teachers and mentors at Columbia University and Yale School of Architecture. But even luckier, I think, is that I grew up in two such utterly different places with such dramatically different forms of architecture. And what I've spent the last ten years or so investigating—and which is the thrust of this book—is how I have been synthesizing those two influences into houses that, to me, feel more American than anything we have ever accomplished before. Bob Stern once counted us among the "modern traditionalists." That has been largely true, at least until recent years, when, I think, we have been trying to modernize traditionalism, to make it feel contemporary, even futuristic at times. Our team has explored the possible and pushed the envelope. And as I have been hybridizing the lessons of New England with the lessons of New Mexico—one could say of blending the Pilgrims and the Puebloan vernacular—my viewpoint has evolved and deepened.

Our buildings, whether they are sited on a spit of land in Massachusetts or a suburban lot in Texas, have begun to feel more vital and more dynamic. They are more experimentally shaped and more consciously sculptural, even to the point of abstraction. The chimneys of our houses, for example, have become triangular where they used to be rectangular, blade-shaped features that seem to be slicing through a roof rather than emerging from it. Columns echo that angularity. Straightforward window and door openings are now recessed, often dramatically so, just as walls that used to be plumb have begun to flare out, like peplums; front doors are largely hidden from view to maximize engagement and mystery. Corners are being chamfered, and overhangs, in some cases, have a pagoda-like upward swoop—which, neatly enough, harks back to the shingle style, which absorbed influences from the popular Japan Pavilion at the 1876 Centennial International Exposition in Philadelphia.

Most of the houses that we have built since we founded our practice in 1989 have been essays in the classic shingle style, compositions of wood frames and cedar shingles, redolent of the buildings of my childhood. They have been admired, and for that praise, we are grateful. But if we did not challenge ourselves creatively, there would be no forward movement. The architects of the past that we as a firm most admire are those who have twisted tradition in order to reinvent it, to make it new again.

Three decades into my architectural career, I have realized, somewhat ironically, that American architecture is about individuality of expression. Recognizing this takes a long time. Owning a home is the biggest part of the American dream, and not just any home, but a home that expresses everything about you. We are a country of homesteaders, descended from men and women who constructed houses in the wilderness, from the Pilgrims of the seventeenth century on the East Coast to the pioneers who settled the West. American culture is built on the notion of the American home; it is ingrained. It is where we live, where we love, where we raise our families, where we express who we are. It is a three-dimensional embodiment of everything we believe in. Very few Americans are immune to this, which amazes me and inspires me as I begin developing a project and get to know our clients and what their vision of home is. A house should be much more than just a shelter—it is a declaration of independence.

OPPOSITE: *Watercolor of light animating the wall of the Colosseum, Rome.* **TOP**: *Goddards, Sir Edwin Lutyens, 1900–10, Abinger Common, Surrey, England.* **ABOVE**: *A brick and rubble stone spandrel in the arcade at Tigbourne Court, Sir Edwin Lutyens, 1899–1900, Wormley, Surrey, England.*

WOODLAND

upper brookville, new york

RED

The finest shingle style houses, to my mind, amply exhibit the dynamic tension between the earthbound and the airborne, anchorage versus flight. The house that we conjured for clients on the North Shore of Long Island exemplifies that quality, while also mixing into the nineteenth-century architectural recipe strong references to the concurrent English cottage style vocabulary. It is a stylistic hybridization that we have, for obvious reasons, called "shinglish."

This house is steeped in architectural precedent, with an array of details discovered in books in our office library and adapted. The soaring chimneys look back to English arts and crafts architect C. F. A. Voysey but scaled up to balance the horizontality of the house. The tower is a recalibration of one at H. H. Richardson's house for Mary Fiske Stoughton (1883) on Brattle Street in Cambridge. The interior of our house exhibits just as many recast ideas, from flat balusters reminiscent of the designs of Josef Hoffmann to white-oak basket-weave woodwork—thankfully preserved in the Metropolitan Museum of Art—that we modified from the Metcalfe house (1884) in Buffalo by McKim, Mead & White. There is even a column screen that has its roots in Frank Lloyd Wright's Winslow house (1893) in Oak Park.

In the same vein as the dramatic cat-slide roofs that Sir Edwin Lutyens so effectively incorporated in his designs, notably at Folly Farm (1906) in Sulhamstead, England, steeply raked eaves anchor the rambling mass of the Long Island house. Composed of hand-thrown artisanal brick in a tawny shade that is pitched somewhere between red and orange and tightly wrapped in tonally related shingles, the exterior color scheme definitely references Red House, the suburban London residence that Philip Webb designed for arts and crafts maestro William Morris in the late 1850s. Limiting the palette to a single color, as well as suppressing, or even eliminating, the trim accentuates the forms. The Brooklyn Historical Society, completed in 1881 to the designs of George B. Post, is one of my favorite examples, a concerted palette of red brick, red terra-cotta, and red windows. In our design, ruddy hues keep the house separate from the green of the surrounding woodlands.

The materials used in the house are all different, and sunlight affects them in various ways, so the building never appears to be static. The impression is that of a buoyant sculpture being held down so that it does not float away, almost as if the house is composed of interlocking tents. The effect is weightless, but it also broadcasts a protective quality, the roof pulled down to enclose interiors that are unexpectedly filled with sunlight streaming through mullioned windows that fragment the light into sequins.

PRECEDING PAGES: *The red palette allows the multifaceted exterior to coalesce into a single sculptural form.* OPPOSITE: *Baronial in scale but breezy in effect, the main staircase rises from the entrance hall.*

ABOVE: *Shaped balusters in the manner of Josef Hoffmann top panels carved in a basketweave pattern inspired by the work of McKim, Mead & White.*
OPPOSITE: *A column screen separates the dining room from the hall. Glazed double doors lead to the walled parterre.*

A covered walk is completely wrapped with fishscale shingles, a treatment that offers a fanciful contrast to the linear coursing on the facades.

From inflected gables to flared walls, the pool house—conceived in the form of a carriage house—is the main residence in miniature.

ABOVE: *Running bond brickwork contrasts with drunken weave shingling.* **OPPOSITE:** *Asymmetry—here, a truncated gable—amplifies the picturesque impression.*
OVERLEAF: *Red roof and walls stand out against the greens of the lawn and forest.*

ENTRANCE ELEVATION

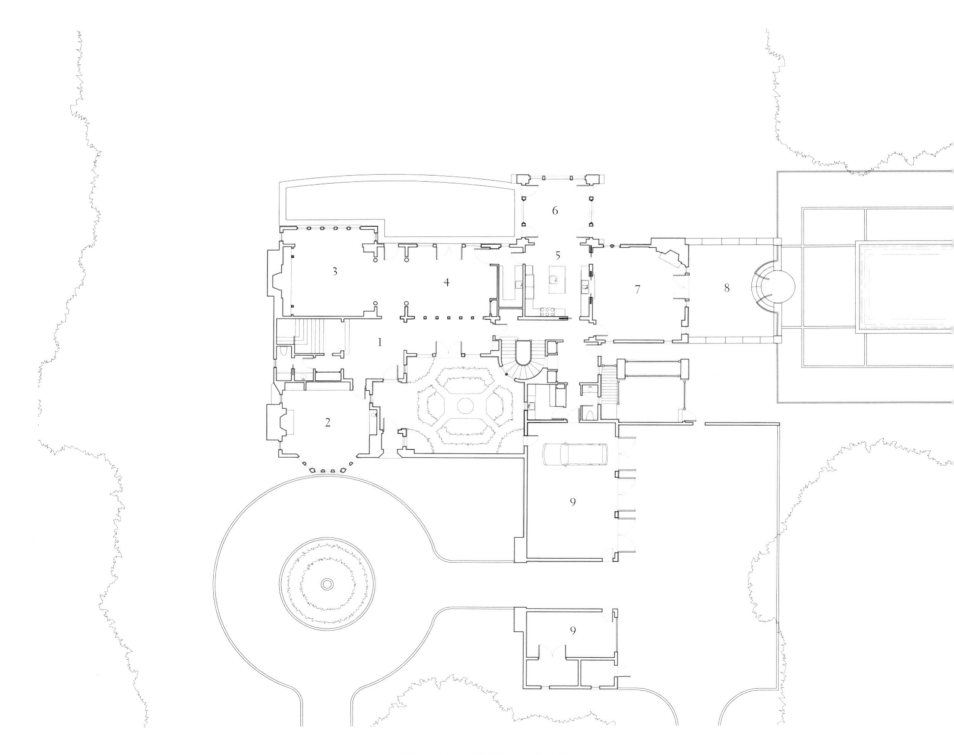

FIRST FLOOR PLAN

first floor

1. Entry
2. Library
3. Living room
4. Dining room
5. Kitchen
6. Breakfast room
7. Family room
8. Terrace
9. Garage
10. Pool House

second floor

11. Stair hall
12. Guest room
13. Primary bedroom
14. Primary bathroom
15. Dressing room

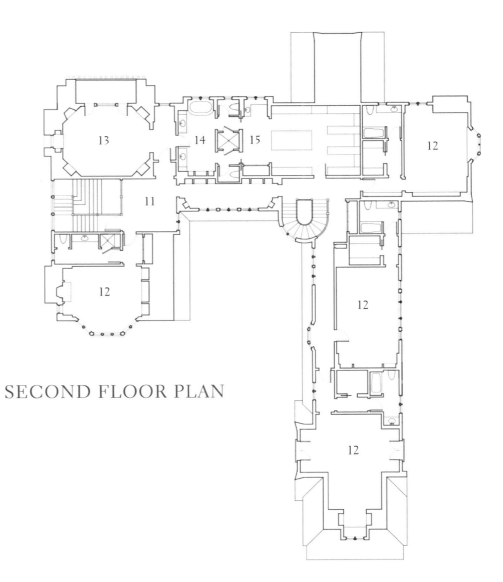

SECOND FLOOR PLAN

ANTHRACITE

lake keowee, south carolina

LODGE

Blending with the surrounding landscape was a cardinal virtue of shingle style architecture for many years. No matter how big the house or how dramatic its massing, the goal was often self-effacement, for the building to take its cues from the trees and rocks into a chromatic vocabulary of green, brown, red, and gray stains. Guidelines for residential architecture on Lake Keowee ensure that houses coexist harmoniously with the thousands of wooded acres, following the lead of early shingle style houses.

For clients who had purchased a hillside property with an extensive waterfront, we developed a long, linear two-story residence fashioned of black-stained cedar clapboard. Like old-fashioned creosote stains, the dark wash is transparent enough that the natural wood shows through. It is also dense enough to allow the house and its garage/guest quarters to stand their ground; a heroic pergola serves as the open passage between the neighboring structures.

The wood cladding that we specified is unexpectedly bold. Since the black stain causes the building to recede from view, we exaggerated the profile of the materials to give the architecture a stronger sculptural presence. Given the landscape, the details are mountain scale: the wide clapboards are more than an inch thick at the outer edges, and the cedar shakes on the roofs even heartier. But the house does not feel blocky. Chamfered corners and windows soften the mass, and the roofs spread wide and proclaim shelter, harking back to the soulful, blanket-like roofs of Frank Lloyd Wright and Sir Edwin Lutyens.

The chimneys are varied as well, the central one being a diamond, the flankers being triangular; all are capped with lead-coated copper and accented by projecting razor-like bands. A low Richardsonian arch, partially glazed, signals the entrance, an opening wrapped in staggered white-oak bands that funnel indoors in a telescoping perspective.

The coal-dark house looks from a distance a bit like a locomotive traveling through the trees, while the curving footprint, following the contours of the land, offers radiating viewpoints from within. Though brooding on the outside, the interiors of the structure are light and sunny, the palette gold rather than anthracite. Largely untreated white oak dresses the entrance hall, colonnade, and living/dining area—ceilings as well as walls—in a variety of patterns, from simple to complex. Like a shingle style house turned inside out, the scheme was sparked by our interest in the work of Henri Jacques Le Même, a Swiss architect of the 1920s and 1930s, who was known for exaggerated chalets in a style that might be called "Alpine art deco." Pilasters and columns are inset with panels of overlapping diamonds, while the walls and the tapering chimneys are striped with decorative horizontal motifs ranging from zigzagging to arrowheads. The interlocking patterns are cozy, warm, and textured—as if the rooms had been knitted and stitched rather than cut and sawn, an Alpine embrace in the New World.

PRECEDING PAGES: *A dark stain, resembling old-fashioned creosote, gives the house a sculptural impression while also allowing it to recede into the landscape.* OPPOSITE: *A 1920s ski resort in Megève, France, designed by architect Henri Jacques Le Même, inspired the treatment of the main floor. The white-oak paneled walls and ceilings suggest the patterns of cable-knit sweaters.* OVERLEAF: *Diamond-paneled columns punctuate the main corridor; the staircase is enclosed in corrugated millwork.*

Dynamic diagonal striping, also inspired by Le Même's work in the French Alps, expresses the rise of the stair.

The double-height living area features an open kitchen at one end. The cabinets and appliances, marble counter, and patinated hood bring the exterior palette indoors.

Grandly scaled chimneys anchor the house to the site;
their monumentality is expressed inside as well as out.

OPPOSITE: *Clerestory windows bring additional light into the interior while also throwing the paneling into deeper relief.* **ABOVE:** *Exaggerated profiles cast deeper, more emphatic shadows inside and out.* **OVERLEAF:** *A preliminary sketch illustrates the way the project would follow the slope of the land.*

RIGHT: *The primary entrance is framed by a broad arch that alludes to the designs of H. H. Richardson and to the carved adobe forms of the Southwest.*
OVERLEAF: *Massive battered piers support a pergola that marks the entrance to the gravel court.*

54

OPPOSITE: *The slats of pergola cast bold shadows over the path between the residence and guest quarters/garage.* **ABOVE:** *Rows of clapboard, aligned with the muntins, emphasize the horizontality of the building.* **OVERLEAF:** *The arch that frames the pool is an echo of the main entrance, just as the freeform water feature evokes the contours of Lake Keowee.*

ABOVE: *Interior woodwork details include diamond-pattern shingles and carved bands.* **OPPOSITE AND OVERLEAF:** *The rambling house was designed to be nestled within the wooded site and almost hidden from view.*

FIRST FLOOR PLAN

WATERFRONT ELEVATION

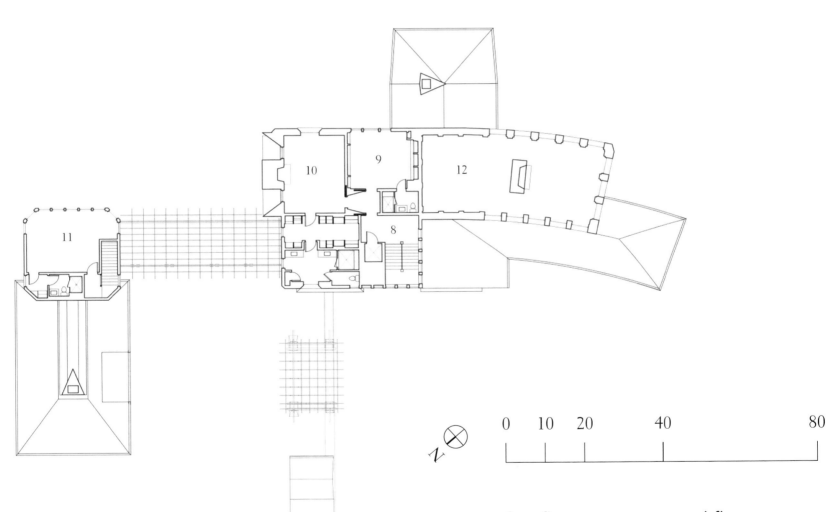

SECOND FLOOR PLAN

0   10   20   40   80

first floor

1. Entry
2. Living/Dining
3. Kitchen
4. Screened porch
5. Guest room
6. Gardening shed
7. Garage

second floor

8. Stair hall
9. Library
10. Primary suite
11. Guest room
12. Open to below

SHINGLE

martha's vineyard

DUNE

massachusetts

GABLE

Shipwrights had a hand in many old houses in New England, and very often they constructed roofs that bowed, as if they were building the hull of a ship upside down. This house on Martha's Vineyard alludes to that vernacular, especially to the bowed gables of Tenacre, a 1920s shingle style house in Southampton by John Russell Pope. It is a protective sheltering shape.

Since our house is set on a dune, just a short walk from the water's edge, the design—inside and out—is informed by the past, when a house beside the sea did not attempt urban perfection. The birch planks that span the ground-floor ceilings were whitewashed before they were installed; the joints have become irregular as the boards moved and settled in. The floorboards were similarly untreated, the reclaimed driftwood left slightly rough and a bit uneven, just lightly sanded smooth. Matter-of-fact, too, are the wall treatments on the main level, where reclaimed timber framing is inset with painted flat paneling or, in the case of a small reading nook with a sloped ceiling, sheets of sound-muffling cork arranged into chevrons.

Traditional on the outside and contemporary within, marrying the tastes of each half of the couple, the house is a very horizontal structure. It lounges across the dune like a blanket spread out for a picnic, following the natural contours of the ground. Relaxed, episodic buildings are what I'm drawn to, their sense of ease with themselves and their surroundings.

Shingle style summer cottages from the 1880s frequently have thin walls, as little as four inches thick, largely because they were not used in cold weather. Here, they are often two feet thick, so the house feels sturdy and protective. Twin chimneys—red brick whitened with a slurry of mortar—are exposed indoors, where they frame a reclaimed oak staircase that passes through a radiating brick vault as it makes its way up to the bedroom level.

Curves play a major role, though they are not immediately obvious, from the convex gables to the concave dormers that flare out to meld with the shingled roofs. In one guest room, the ceiling curves as it follows the bowed roof. Some of the exterior columns, which are very simple and purposefully under-detailed, flare at the top, echoing the shape of the dormers but in reverse, so they meld with the ceiling and appear to carry weight rather than being merely decorative.

The house is a porous and sculptural building, a single, long volume perforated by a range of windows from small casements to triple-hung sash. A broad breezeway cuts through the house, as do several deep porches. These transitional spaces are painted white in a deliberate departure from the earth tones of the shingle style. It is a fresh, contemporary gesture that suggests that the building has a snowy core that has been revealed beneath the shingle skin.

We took a more modern approach to the pool house. It is a bubble of steel and glass that has been wrapped in teak slats, its lightness serving as a foil to the solidity of the main house—as if the smaller structure was going to be clad in shingles but instead was left in a strikingly transparent state.

PRECEDING PAGES: *Massive chimneys dominate the roofline of this house of otherwise traditional shingled mien.* OPPOSITE: *Usually seen in the American South, triple-hung windows open the house to the landscape; the muntins are mirrored by the flat paneling on the walls.* OVERLEAF: *Unpainted beams cross the beadboard ceiling of the porch, suggesting that the room was once an enclosed space that was opened up during a renovation.*

ABOVE: *An open porch is supported by tapered columns and softly shaped openings that frame the landscape.* OPPOSITE: *A variety of profiles—rounded, angular, inset—sculpt the ceiling and walls of an upper landing.*

The family staircase wraps around the base of a chimney, which has been extended with a scooped arch. A pale slurry of mortar coats the red bricks.

OPPOSITE: *Another staircase is conceived as an envelope of wood with board paneling that emphasizes the height of the space.* ABOVE: *A herringbone cork wallcovering quiets the inglenook.* OVERLEAF: *The pool house at night, as seen across the neighboring dune.*

PRECEDING PAGES: *The pool house recalls a deconstructed shed.* ABOVE AND OPPOSITE: *Wood slats enclose the glass pool house, casting shadows that stripe the interior.*

LEFT: *The exterior slats are expressed inside as a horizontally channeled wood wall.* OVERLEAF: *Pocket doors slide open to a view of the pool and the sea beyond.*

89

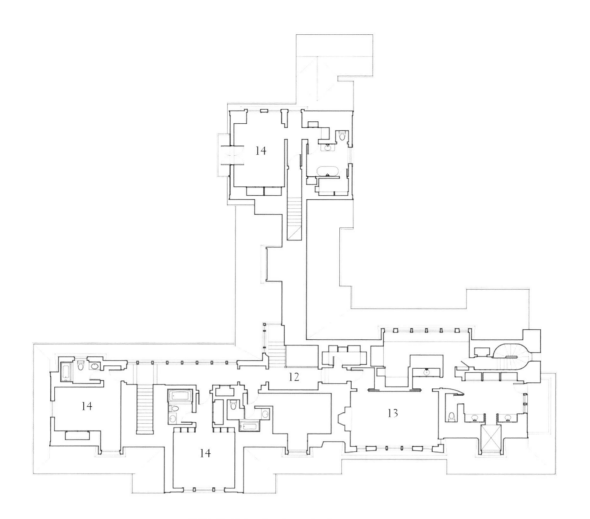

SECOND FLOOR PLAN

0   10   20   40   80

N

first floor

1. Entry
2. Living room
3. Study
4. Inglenook
5. Kitchen
6. Breakfast
7. Family room
8. Screened porch
9. Breezeway
10. Garage
11. Gardening shed

second floor

12. Stair hall
13. Primary suite
14. Guest room

FIRST FLOOR PLAN

WATERFRONT ELEVATION

CURVE

water mill

LOUVER

new york

PORCH

Porches are an integral component of shingle style houses, offering opportunities for plein-air living and protection from the elements. They can also lighten the bulk of a building, being open, transparent volumes rather than conventionally enclosed rooms.

The porches we integrated into a shingled house on Long Island transform it into a multilayered exploration of indoor–outdoor living. A screened porch is tucked into a low gable near the front of the house; a covered porch is intended for barbecuing and dining; another covered porch spans the rear elevation facing the bay. Most dramatic is the porch on the upper floor, which leads to a descending breezeway that becomes porch-like with its slat walls. This quirky stepped element is capped by louvered monitors.

The house blends various architectural influences of the past, but the sources are mixed carefully. The shingle style informs the exterior, very much expanding on the Stanford White mode, while the spare, bright interior channels International Style modernism. This aesthetic juxtaposition melds with subtle curves that pull away from or inwardly embrace the rectilinear forms as the footprint of the house twists and turns. The pink-brick chimneys and skinny porch columns can be traced to White's Isaac Bell house (1883) in Newport, Rhode Island, one of my favorite buildings. The Bell house also includes sliding panels that open up the rooms for an uninterrupted flow; here, we installed sliding screens and glass doors that glide into the exterior walls, so the ground floor can be opened as broadly as possible, becoming in some ways a porch within a porch.

Some of the roof terminations have pagoda-like points that swoop six or seven feet into the air. People have commented that they have a Japanese air, but they were the result of the sweep of my pen. When you allow your subconscious to direct your hand as you draw, serendipitous details emerge that you would not do if you were thinking about them. The same process resulted in the tapering star-shape columns, which are basically square columns that have been carved out to capture shadow and light.

Vincent Scully once wrote that "the essential objective of the shingle style was the creation of expanding space, vertically pointed and horizontally stretched." The Water Mill house does precisely that, but it also incorporates a subtle nod to a Borromini spirit. More and more of our houses are curved like this one. While living in Rome during my sabbatical at the American Academy, I spent hours sketching on morning walks and meditative afternoons with my Papiers d'Arches paper and watercolor palette, absorbing the sunlit Roman ruins. I came to appreciate how curves allow for a sense of the passing of the day by emphasizing the effect of sunlight, how a curve invites shadows in an ever-changing panorama.

Throughout the house, the building curves—a bit like a sail filled with a breeze. There is always a slightly different view of the bay; the pool follows that curve, as do the limestone floors and the glossy white plank ceilings—all like architectural sound waves.

PRECEDING PAGES: *This house is a contemporary exploration of classic shingle style, anchored by hefty tapering chimneys and distinguished by broad, flared gables.*
OPPOSITE: *Porch columns have faceted profiles and elongated brackets.*

OPPOSITE: *A sense of streamlined movement is conjured through the application of linear patterns on floor, walls, ceilings, and the staircase enclosure.* OVERLEAF: *The luminous main living area opens to porches on two sides.*

ABOVE: *The gentle curve of the house can be sensed in the paving of an upper porch and in its board ceiling.* OPPOSITE: *Nautical railings edge the main staircase.*

The inner wall of the entrance walk is flared at the base and punctuated by deeply set windows and boldly angled sills, a nod to the adobe forms of the Southwest but executed in wood.

OPPOSITE: *An exterior staircase is sheltered by a series of light monitors that are walled with slats.* OVERLEAF: *A dynamic architectural composition—slatted light monitor, a parade of windows, the curving roof of the entrance walk—can be viewed from the upper porch.*

ABOVE: *A boardwalk skirts the edge of the property and leads to the dock.* OPPOSITE: *One of the gables ends in a pagoda-like swoop. The wall below flares out as if bearing the weight of the house.* OVERLEAF: *The rear terrace overlooks the pool and the bay beyond.* SECOND OVERLEAF: *Like the house, the retaining wall of the stone pool terrace traces a long curve.*

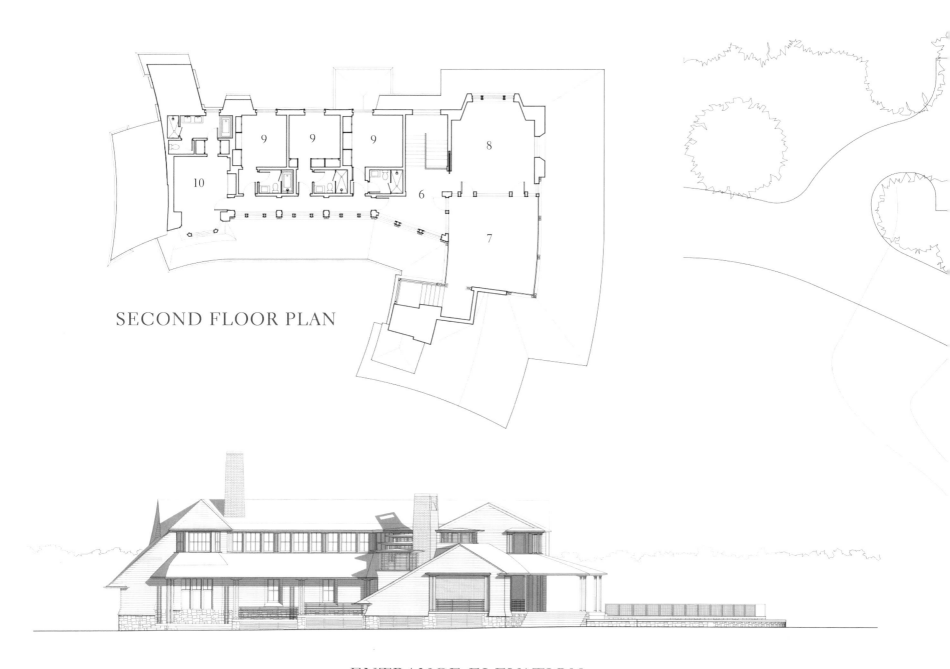

SECOND FLOOR PLAN

ENTRANCE ELEVATION

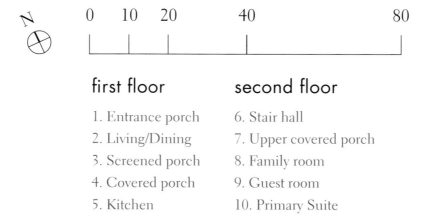

N

0   10   20   40   80

first floor

1. Entrance porch
2. Living/Dining
3. Screened porch
4. Covered porch
5. Kitchen

second floor

6. Stair hall
7. Upper covered porch
8. Family room
9. Guest room
10. Primary Suite

FIRST FLOOR PLAN

ORIGAMI

sagaponack

FLARE

new york

LOFT

Shingle style architecture does not have a strict vocabulary, aside from the primary building material. The picturesque irregularities of the 1880s encouraged experimentation rather than rigidity, back when practitioners such as Bruce Price and Wilson Eyre were setting daring precedents in terms of volume and silhouettes. The idiosyncrasies of that period, though, have been ironed out over the last century or so, and our office is always looking to the past to find a way forward. How much can we push the envelope? How abstract can we get without losing the qualities that people love about the shingle style?

After completing a shingle style house in Sagaponack, we were invited to design a guest house on land separated from the original site by a stone path. The smaller structure echoes the main building in material (cedar shingles), fenestration (diamond-pane windows), trim (white-painted wood), and details (classical dentils, doors with grids of glass). There is even a staircase with timber treads and a steel meander balustrade, a simpler version of the complex stair in the main house. But the guest house is not a pocket-size mirror image. The primary residence is a respectful contemporary exploration of classic shingle style, while the four-bedroom guest house is whimsical, with a bit of a mannerism in its DNA. It is even turned upside down, with bedrooms on the ground floor (triple-hung windows allow visitors to walk straight outdoors). A wide, open living area takes over the upper level, where a massive picture window frames dramatic views of dunes and ocean.

At either end of the building are bold gables that appear to be folded and creased like paper or starched linen. Their profile recalls everything from women's headdresses of the early sixteenth century to the kabuto helmets worn by samurai—a possible source of inspiration for Price and his architectural brethren, given the pervasive Asian influences in that era. Fanned, overlapped, set on the diagonal, and installed in waves, the shingles have been laid to emphasize the angled planes of the gables. The combination gives the impression that the guest house is in motion and being hit with a strobe light.

Virtually nothing about the exterior of the guest house is straight. The lower-floor walls tilt back while flaring out over the stone foundation, as if the house is being stretched by tent pegs. The walls may not be plumb, but the windows are, which results in deep windowsills and a sense of the openings being sliced out of the building.

Putting the living/dining area on the upper floor gave us an opportunity to shape the space as distinctively as we did the exterior. Two-inch-wide maple strips have been joined into a ceiling that seems to drift from one side of the room to the other: clean and modern but unorthodox. It is an abstract reference to the vast open lofts where sailmakers laid out yards of white canvas. The roll of the ceiling recalls clouds, sea swells, even the billow of a mainsail.

PRECEDING PAGES: *The shaped and folded gable suggests a traditional samurai helmet.* OPPOSITE: *A stone path between the primary residence, at left, and the guest house leads to the lawn and the dunes.*

Inflected planes give the impression that the walls of guest house have been folded like origami paper.

OPPOSITE: *Colonial revival details, such as lattice windows and brackets, from the main residence reappear on the guest house, though its tilted planes create a sense of movement.* **OVERLEAF, LEFT:** *The kitchen resembles a ship's galley.* **OVERLEAF, RIGHT:** *The inflected angles on the exterior are echoed in the travertine mantel in the loft-like living space.*

ABOVE: *The treads of the staircase line up with grooves in the walls.* OPPOSITE: *A proscenium-like arch frames the staircase at one end of the living space.*

RIGHT: *Sails and clouds inspired the curved wood ceiling in the loft-like living space.* OVERLEAF: *A terrace, centered with a firepit, stretches across the rear of the guest house.*

ROAD ELEVATION

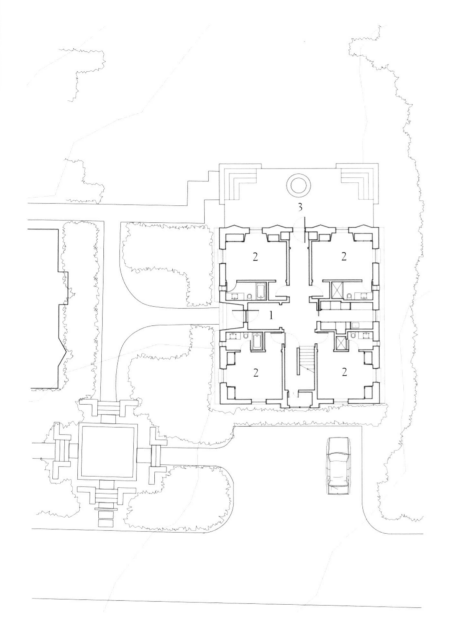

FIRST FLOOR PLAN

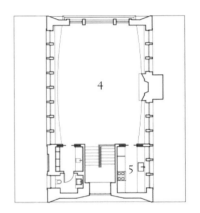

SECOND FLOOR PLAN

0   10   20   40   80

⊗
N

first floor

1. Entry
2. Guest room
3. Terrace

second floor

4. Living/dining loft
5. Kitchen

SILVERED

east hampton, new york

RHYTHM

Every architect I know reveres the 1887 William G. Low house, a masterwork by Charles McKim, now demolished. For clients in East Hampton, it was our touchstone.

Like its predecessor, our building reads as one earthbound gable encased in shingles. But it is not, because we sliced McKim's gable concept at the center to create separate points. McKim's daring design led us to develop a similarly sculptural yet more muscular building with separate experiences: a multi-dimensional main facade displaying signature shingle style attributes with the entrance discreetly tucked in, and a rear facade that offers a warm welcome to family and friends.

From the street, the house appears as a dynamic composition of thrusting triangles, hexagonal dormers that serve as light monitors, and hearty, inflexed chimneys capped with bead-blasted stainless steel. We like chimneys to have the effect of spears or nails, as if they have fallen from the sky, pierced the roof, and been driven into the earth. They should appear to literally anchor the building.

Gentle counterpoints temper the angularity of the jagged skyline. Barely perceptible hoods peep over the windows and louvered vents, all of which seem to have been pushed into the body of the building. The parade of windows over the entrance, which brings sunlight into the staircase's upper landing, has a flared base. The siding is simple: no diamond patterns, no fish scales. Just matter-of-fact shingles doing their job.

The interior reverses the gray shingled, white-windowed exterior with soft white plaster walls and dark floorboards. Moldings and baseboards seem to have been pressed into the walls; the marble and onyx trim is set flush with the plaster walls; ceilings here and there are framed with broad, low-profile details that radiate like the surf. This architecture is not about tacking disparate elements into place; for us, it is about subtracting.

The entrance stair hall is an exception: here the moldings project rather than recede, wrapping around the two-story space. The staircase pierces a tripartite screen along the west wall of this entryway, with bronze stair railings connecting to the second-floor balustrade—think of it as a tarnished-gold cage—adding an organic texture bearing witness to the fact that each baluster has been shaped by hand.

An idea that has its roots in Lutyens is the path of discovery through the rooms, which do not unfold in a logical way. The best view is rarely a straight line. Large rooms collapse into small ones that lead into medium spaces; ceiling heights shift. There is always a sense of surprise, and the sensation that the house is tempting you onward. The end of that journey is the back of the house. It is more traditional than the main facade, with a bluestone terrace opening to a lush lawn beautifully landscaped. It is a much easier read: shutters, windows, rhythms. The emotional reaction that it sparks is universal: a home that is warm and embracing, a domestic hearth that embodies the fourth dimension of architecture explained by Grosvenor Atterbury as "where it is not so much a matter of seeing as feeling."

PRECEDING PAGES: *The split and secondary gables on the entrance facade extend the traditional shingle style vocabulary while the deeply recessed windows and boldly shaped chimneys allude to the monumental forms of the Southwest.* OPPOSITE: *The low entrance porch and modest front door, on the right, open into a double-height entrance hall.*

ABOVE: *Glazed doors flank a window intended to frame the garden like a painting.* **OPPOSITE:** *The staircase is tucked to one side of the entrance hall, allowing the space to be understood as a single, uninterrupted volume.*

Anchored by a minimalist stone mantel, gridded panels of rift white oak span the fireplace wall of the living room.

Another grid, this one composed of parchment blocks, wraps the walls of the double-height study.

Projections and overhangs work with deeply recessed openings to animate the taut shingled surfaces.

ABOVE, OPPOSITE, AND OVERLEAF: *The garden side of the house is filled with family and entertaining spaces, including an elegant pergola by the tennis court and a generous bluestone terrace.* **PAGES 158–59:** *One of the working sketches for the project.* **PAGES 160–61:** *A gazebo-like pool house overlooks the far end of the swimming pool.*

ENTRANCE ELEVATION

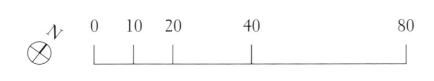

0   10   20   40   80

first floor

1. Entry
2. Living room
3. Dining room
4. Kitchen
5. Breakfast room
6. Family room
7. Screened porch
8. Study
9. Library
10. Primary suite
11. Garage

second floor

12. Stair hall
13. Open to below
14. Guest room

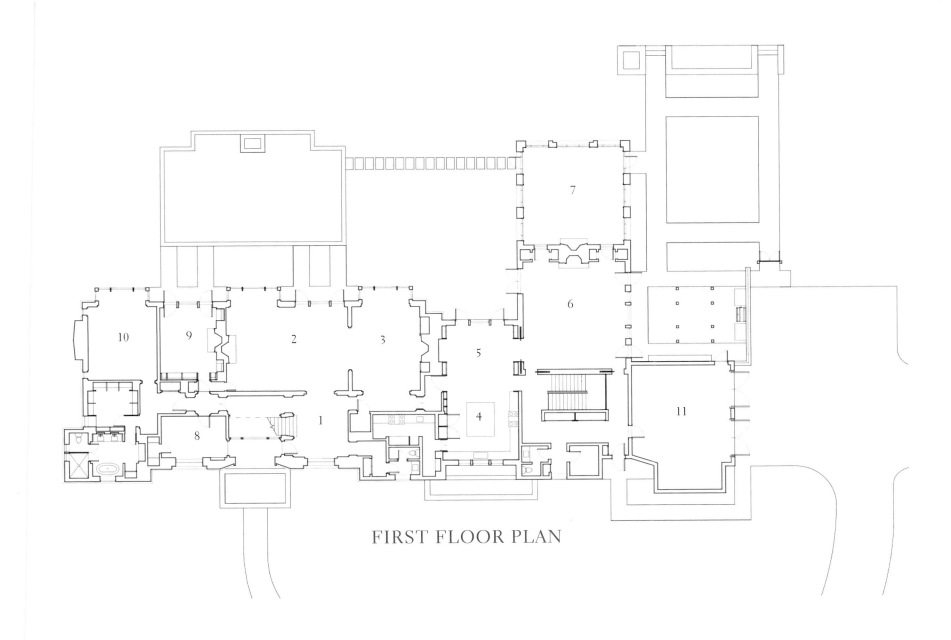

FIRST FLOOR PLAN

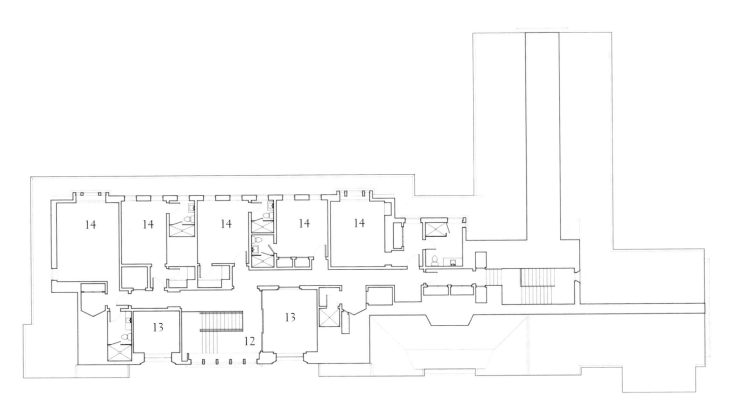

SECOND FLOOR PLAN

STEEL

seattle

GLASS

washington

FOREST

The house that we designed in a forest setting in the Pacific Northwest is all about honesty. By that I mean that there is no ornamentation that is not an essential part of the actual structure; the decoration is the structural system. It is a building that does not hide anything, and, in fact, the design philosophy was to celebrate what is essential. The materials express precisely what they are: wood, metal, concrete, and glass. The sloping roof is made of standing-seam zinc, which needs no finish, while the exterior of the house is an asymmetrical composition of board-formed concrete and shou sugi ban, horizontal boards of cedar wood that, in Japanese fashion, have been charred, burnished, and sealed. The leaders and gutters are unfinished metal, and soffits are raw hemlock.

Though this philosophy is one that is associated with shingle style architecture, where no structural aspect of the building is entirely obscured, this is most obviously not a shingle style house. It is lean, it is spare, it is reductive, and perhaps most significant, it is largely transparent.

Very few openings interrupt the primary facade: a sliver of clerestory window on the upper level, a front door tucked into the right angle and protected by a cantilevered visor, and a doorway in an extended concrete wall that leads to the side yard and a fire pit. The rear of the house opens up to the landscape, a 25-foot-high stainless-steel curtain wall of teak-framed glass that overlooks the forest. Here, too, structural requirements provide the ornament, namely a two-story screen of huge interlocking I-beams—our tip of the hat to the work of Mies van der Rohe—that support the roof overhang and frame the view in interesting ways. Because of the curtain wall, the house is at one with the forest that wraps around it, and its multitude of vertical elements echo the trees that are an integral aspect of the property. The landscape is rarely out of sight and thus becomes part of how the house and its rooms are experienced.

The material honesty of the exterior is expressed indoors as well; everything is exposed for what it is and what it does. Douglas fir glulams support the roof, and fumed oak panels the walls. Steel in a gunmetal shade frames the curtain wall, and the same material has been used as a fireplace surround in the double-height living area. Where the walls are plaster, the color has been integrated. The floors are made of tadelakt, waterproof polished plaster traditionally employed in Moroccan hammams. It has a soft solidity that evokes the buildings of the American Southwest that have influenced me from childhood.

The overall impression of the house, indoors and out, is a kind of smokiness, a palette of natural tones that is very well suited to the Pacific Northwest.

PRECEDING PAGES: *A screen of black I-beams creates a gallery of woodland views from the interior of the house.* OPPOSITE: *Materials in the living area—a ceiling of untreated hemlock planks, the patinated steel superstructure, and walnut-framed windows—are carefully orchestrated to complement the forest setting.*

ABOVE: *The staircase's zigzag treads are offset by a screen of horizontal slats.* **OPPOSITE:** *A board-formed concrete wall backs a dining terrace.*

ABOVE: *An intersection of linear patterns—from the board-formed concrete walls to the slatted screen—establishes a serene atmosphere in the entrance vestibule.*
OPPOSITE: *Untreated hemlock lines the soffits of the entrance porch.* OVERLEAF: *Preliminary sketch.*

The terrace on the rear of the house is tucked between two I-beam screens that extend from the foundation to the roofline.

ABOVE: *The staircase is a dramatic passage between walls paneled with horizontal planks.* **OPPOSITE:** *Layers of framing—patinated steel indoors and an I-beam screen outdoors—fragment the landscape into a kaleidoscope of images.* **OVERLEAF:** *The strong horizontals of the vestibule contrast with the soaring verticality of the living space.*

The opening in the fumed-oak wall at the end of the living area leads to the kitchen, which features a minimalist walnut island and expansive window that overlooks the forest.

A corner of the interior offers a catalog of the materials that were used in the project—fumed-oak and hemlock planks, patinated steel, and board-formed concrete—to complement the natural setting.

ABOVE: *The glass wall on the rear of the house reflects both the column screen and the forest.* **OPPOSITE:** *The stone terrace and firepit are enveloped by trees.*
OVERLEAF: *The house becomes a lantern when night falls, a sculpture in light, glass, and steel.*

FOREST ELEVATION

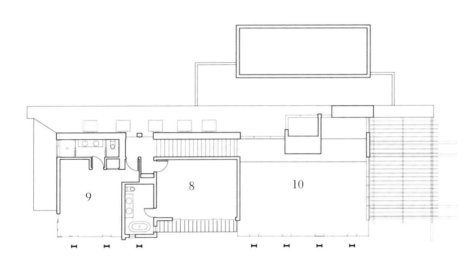

9   8   10

SECOND FLOOR PLAN

N   0   10   20   40   80

first floor

1. Entry
2. Living/Dining
3. Terrace
4. Kitchen
5. Breakfast porch
6. Guest suite
7. Garage

second floor

8. Bunk room
9. Primary suite
10. Open to below

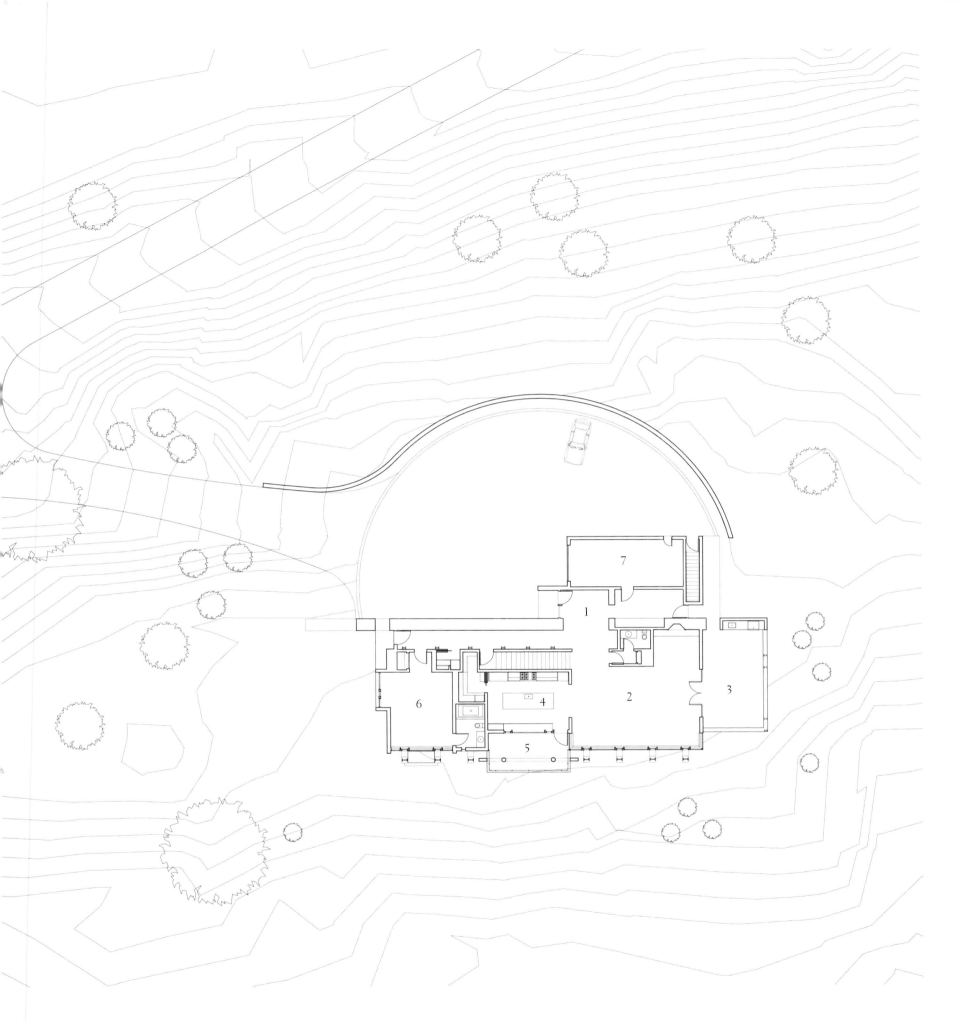

FIRST FLOOR PLAN

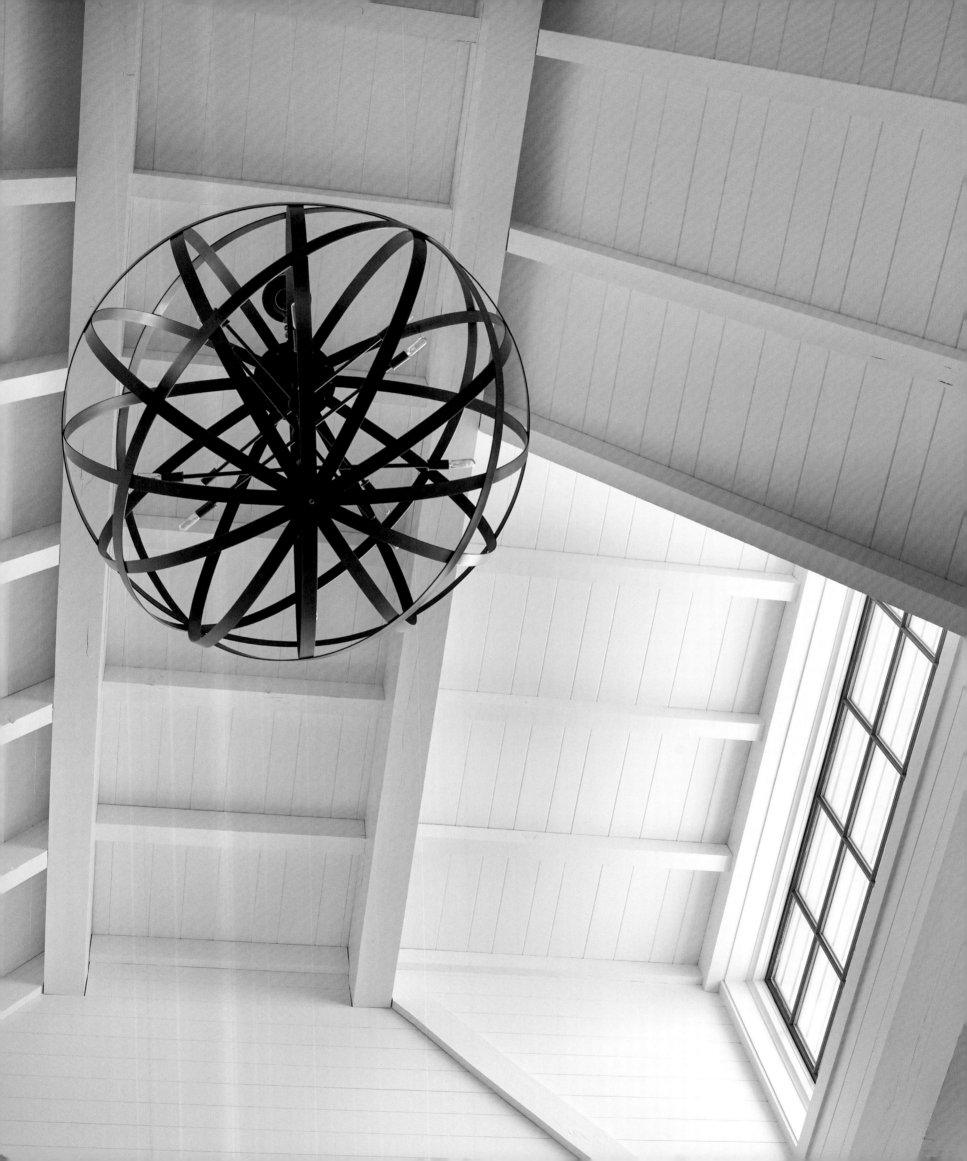

FOLDED

watch hill

GEOMETRIES

rhode island

COVE

Carving is a word we often use when conceptualizing a house, largely because our approach is akin to that of a sculptor faced with a chunk of marble and a chisel. We followed that line of thinking when we were asked to design a seaside house on a point of land in Rhode Island. Flood plain restrictions, a complicated polygonal building area, and a lot surrounded by water on three sides determined the footprint to a significant degree. Basically, we had just enough land to insert an elongated volume, raised above grade, that could only be so wide and so tall. We had to approach that volume as if it were a cardboard box of a fixed size, slicing into it and then folding the flaps in, down, and out, as if we were engaged in the creation of a giant work of origami. It is a creative concept that our designers return to time and again as we approach shaping a house, seeing it as less an act of construction and more an exploration of sculpture.

We did not want the house to look like it was built in the 1880s, though aspects of it are informed by precedents. The jutting visors owe a debt to Ernest Coxhead, an inventive British architect who practiced in the Bay Area at the end of the nineteenth century. The lack of conventional exterior trim and moldings is influenced by the work of John Calvin Stevens, namely Stonecroft, an 1890s house in Maine that was startlingly modern for its time, with pure volumes and sharply articulated planes. We did not want to call out the windows with a contrasting trim color either. Instead, they were painted a medium gray to match the cedar shingles as they weathered, ensuring that the entire house is a uniform color with an abstracted presence.

Like a boat sailing into the cove, the house is a strongly horizontal structure conceived as decks, with dramatically sloping gables and peaks providing verticality; it is a house that rises as much as it spreads. Multiple exposures and triple-hung windows bring in light, air, and transparency, as do numerous porches, both covered and screened.

Horizontal planks and louvers—including those that frame a powerful arch that is carved out of the lower section of the eastern elevation to allow any flood waters to flow below the house—wrap the ground level, seamlessly fading into the shingle courses. The railings follow the coursing as well. These parallel lines rise from the ground to the roof, uninterrupted, the shingles following the gables, dressing the roof, and wrapping the chimneys, which tower like smokestacks on a Gilded Age yacht. On the south elevation stands a chimney that rises a stunning three-and-a-half stories, visually suggesting a giant mast.

That maritime sensibility is carried, with a light hand, indoors. Horizontally channeled wood walls are coated with marine paint; most are white, but the office and den are a deep blue-green that almost looks black. Oak flooring runs the length of the house in the main rooms, further emphasizing the horizontality and carrying the eye out to the landscape and water beyond. We also incorporated details that shape the interior volumes in unexpected yet barely perceptible ways, such as the inwardly inflected walls of the living room that intersect with an asymmetrical corner fireplace. It is a sculpting that you sense long before you notice it. Once you do become aware of that expressiveness, it impresses on your mind that buildings can be far more than an assemblage of logical boxes. A house can be a sculpture yet still do its job as a domestic haven.

PRECEDING PAGES: *To comply with environmental regulations, this house is elevated above the flood plain, with the living space on the upper two floors.*
OPPOSITE: *The staircase is inspired by one in William Morris's Red House, but greatly simplified and abstracted.*

OPPOSITE: *A hearty Dutch door opens to the entrance hall.* OVERLEAF: *A corner fireplace and angled walls in the living room reflect the architecture's arts and crafts roots but expressed with contemporary clarity.*

PRECEDING PAGES: *Arched openings at either end of the house allow floodwaters to flow beneath the structure, through the garage, and out into the property.*
OPPOSITE: *A preliminary sketch of the gable and chimney.* OVERLEAF: *The narrow end of the house addresses the water like the prow of a ship.*

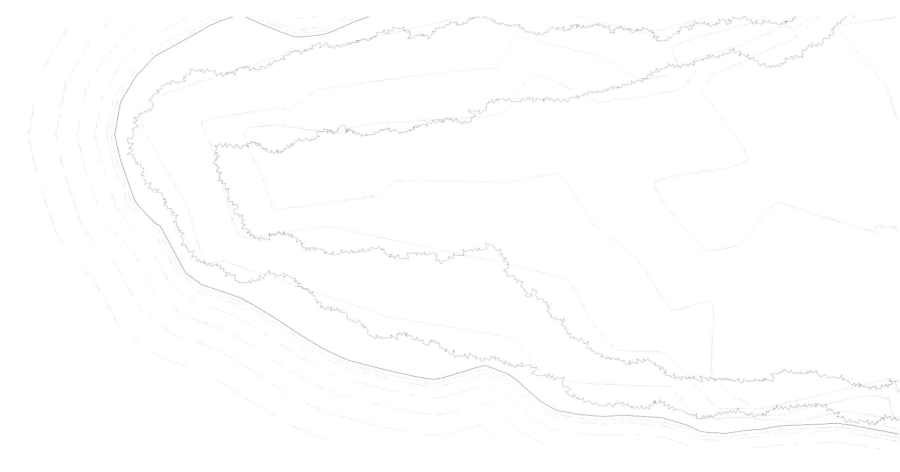

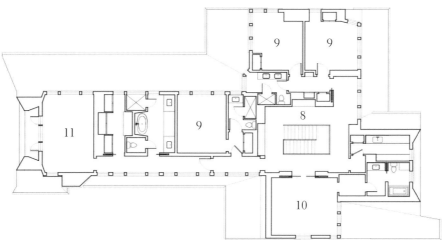

SECOND FLOOR PLAN

⊗ N   0   10   20   40   80

first floor   second floor

1. Entry   8. Stair hall

2. Living/Dining   9. Guest room

3. Kitchen   10. Bunk room

4. Screened porch   11. Primary suite

5. Family room

6. Guest room

7. Porch

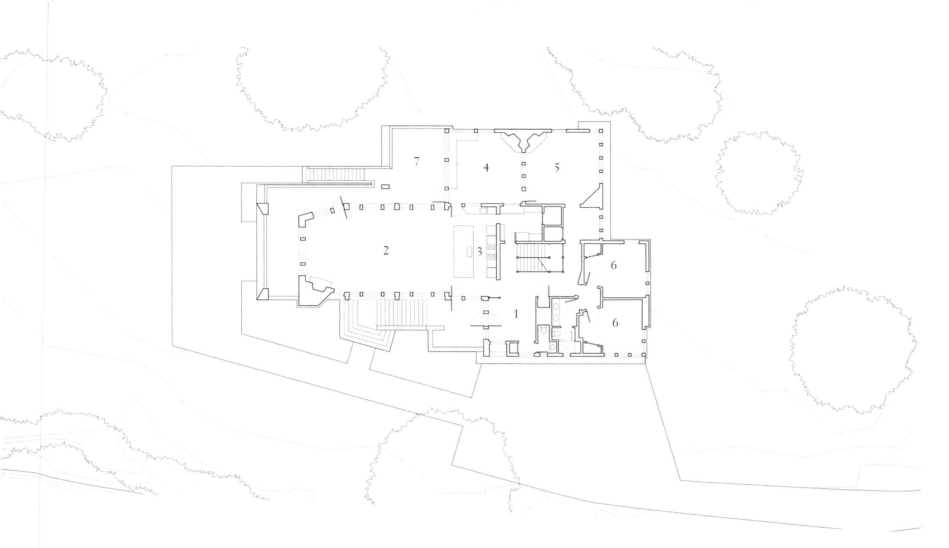

FIRST FLOOR PLAN

ENTRANCE ELEVATION

BLADE

bridgehampton

REFLECTION

new york

MEADOW

The central feature of this house—a blending of contemporary and traditional that our office has been exploring with greater intensity recently—literally came from the notion of a welcoming lantern we saw in an old print. We wanted to express that kind of welcome in the architecture, to build in warmth and spirit in a single structural gesture. Here, that lantern is expressed in a two-story dining room that emerges from the front of the house, walled with glass on two sides and reflected in an L-shape ornamental pool. Imagine arriving for a party, at dusk, and being welcomed by the light of the dining room, mirrored in what amounts to a virtual moat. The effect always makes me think of the Golden Pavilion in Kyoto, a gold-leafed pavilion that sits partially in a pond.

The architecture of this project is one of grand gestures. The dining room may make the biggest impact—it seems to be a glass box floating and reflected in the pool, declaring this house as a contemporary endeavor. But interspersed and contrasting with these glazed gestures are the sharp-edged, taut, unadorned shingled walls and brick chimneys, giving the impression of the simplest buildings that have been sliced open as widely as possible, with some of the openings framed by wide chamfers that add an illusion of depth.

After traversing a covered walkway that skirts the pool, visitors step through the front door into another gesture of unexpected volume: a double-height glazed stair hall that frames the manicured landscape beyond. The main living areas are accessed from this stair hall, arranged across the length of the house in an enfilade of high-ceiling spaces: an expansive living area and bar, the dining room, the family room, and the screened porch with terraces beyond. The living and dining rooms have two exposures, for the light, views of the rest of the house, and ventilation. Transitional spaces extend this level of the house into the landscape. A covered terrace off the living room, and the seasonal screened porch and kitchen overlook an intimate stone courtyard around which the house, pool, and pool house are arranged.

Grand gestures abound in the details as well: the moldings in the entrance hall are gigantic, about three feet wide, while the double-hung windows on the upper level stretch from floor to ceiling and are divided into four big lights. The triangular chimneys are four feet at their widest point and two inches at their narrowest—they seem to be slicing through the house like an ocean liner sailing through a sea—and the columns of the rear terrace mirror that diamond shape. The columns also meld with the terrace roof, which juts straight out from the rear wall of the house at the same time it appears to be extruding the columns themselves. It is a fluid yet refined and razor-sharp gesture in a house where traditional materials are handled with contemporary panache.

One of the virtues of the shingle style is its adaptability. As with the early houses from the 1880s, this house looks forward not backward.

PRECEDING PAGES: *The largely glass rear elevation looks across the lawn to a meadow.* OPPOSITE: *The front door opens to a flying staircase that occupies a glazed pavilion at one end of the building.* OVERLEAF: *A conceptual sketch of the project, with a dining pavilion projecting into an L-shape pool.*

On the terrace, columns are composed of multiple angled elements, see-through supports that cast compelling shadows and reveal intriguing slivers of landscape.

ABOVE: *The entrance to the house is a luminous tunnel-like walkway paneled with wood planks painted gloss black.* **OPPOSITE:** *Blending tradition and modernity, the house, garage, and pool house are wrapped with cedar shingles and inset with painted black elements.*

The stair hall features a glass curtain wall banded in an inflected black frame.

ABOVE: *Flat surfaces give way to gentle angles and soft curves, such as the concave wall of the breakfast room.* OPPOSITE: *Bordered by lavender, a path of bluestone pavers runs between the house and the swimming pool.* OVERLEAF: *A shallow pool borders the double-height dining pavilion, generating complex reflections throughout the day.*

The glazed dining pavilion faces the entrance court and a formal arrangement of London plane trees.

A stately composition of London plane trees, Japanese anemone, and boxwood frames the living room and the pool. The entrance walkway is on the left.

A hydrangea hedge separates the house from the swimming pool area.

233

ABOVE: *Beside the pool, the entrance walkway recalls a stage or a viewing platform.* **OPPOSITE:** *Boxwood hedges line the walkway to the service entrance.*
OVERLEAF: *An allée of London plane trees frames a shingled pool house fronted with a pergola.*

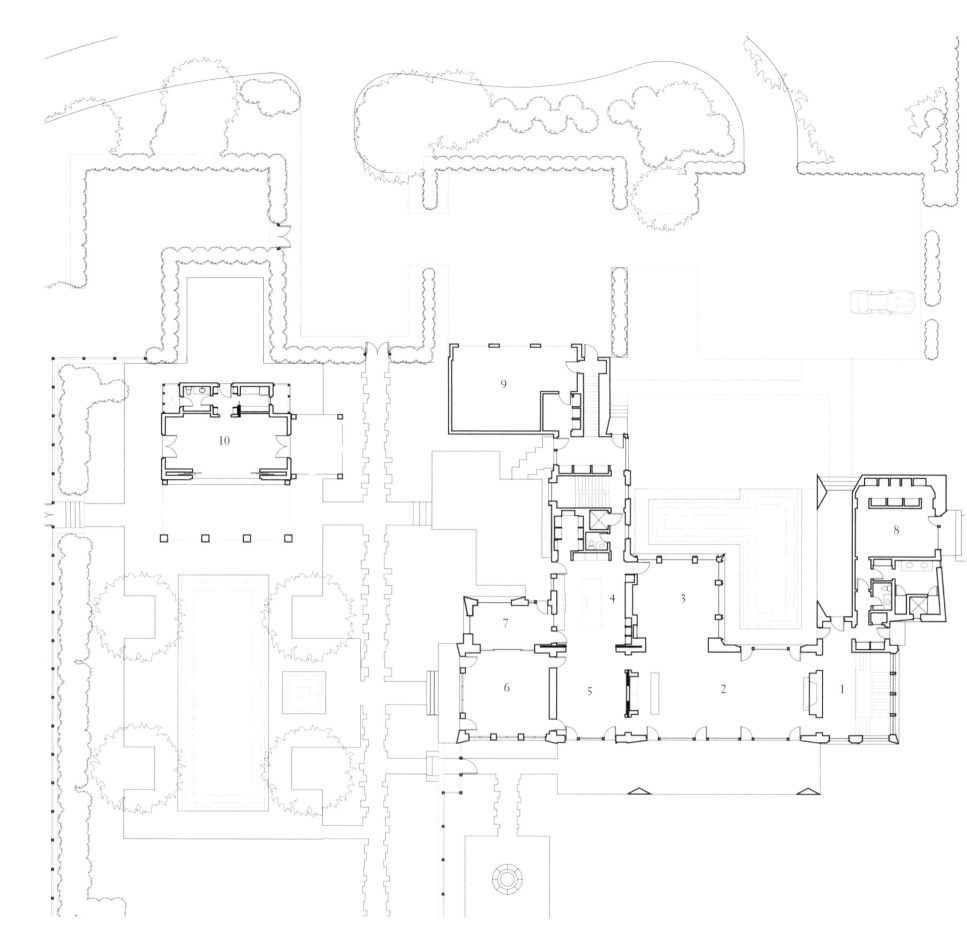

FIRST FLOOR PLAN

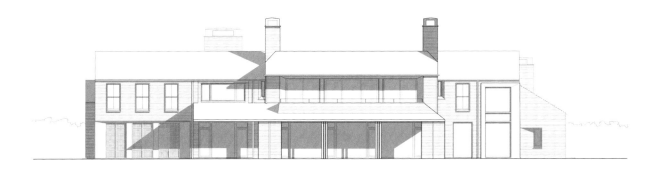

MEADOW ELEVATION

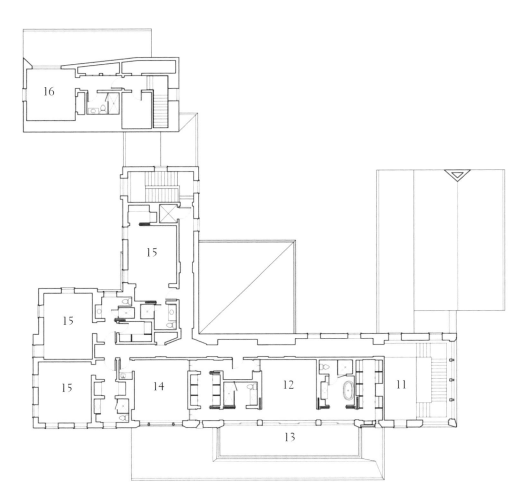

SECOND FLOOR PLAN

N

0   10   20   40   80

first floor

1. Entry
2. Living room
3. Dining room
4. Kitchen
5. Family room
6. Screened porch

7. Breakfast room
8. Guest suite
9. Garage
10. Pool house

second floor

11. Stair hall
12. Primary suite
13. Terrace
14. Sitting room
15. Guest suite
16. Apartment

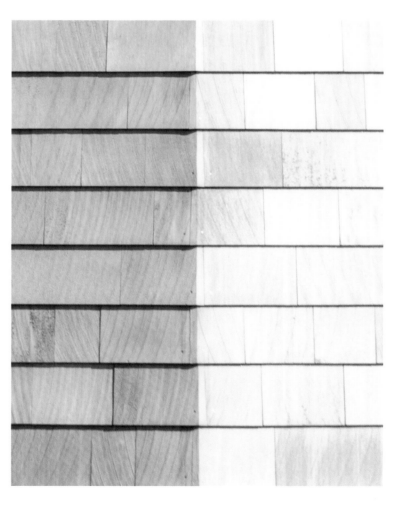

BREAKING

toronto / southampton / dallas / houston

GROUND

A building composed of curves is always more mysterious than a rectilinear box. It reveals itself slowly. The arcing planes seem to suggest a destination that is just out of sight, and then once you reach that point, another curve is there to coax you forward. The anticipatory experience is heightened by the shadows that are cast as sunlight moves across the building's surfaces, beginning as slivers and then expanding into parabolas. There is an unmistakable sense of time unfolding.

Blending curved masses and paper-thin planes and details has become a focus of our work over the last few years. More and more, we juxtapose the airiness of wood construction with the sculptural heft of masonry. To further animate this combination, texture becomes particularly crucial as the form of a building becomes simpler and its details increasingly spare. The more a building is reduced to the absolute basics, the more urgent the need to animate the surfaces that remain, to ensure that they have enough interest, subtle and otherwise—thus our emphasis on textures and how they interact and how they react as the day goes by.

Roofs can appear to billow or slope rakishly to the ground. Walls can present themselves as pillow-soft or as sharp as scythes. Surfaces can be elaborately worked to introduce texture and pattern in stone, brick, shingle, or wood planks. The result is always a house, yes, but one that has the three-dimensionality of a sculpture, supple rather than static. These are the compositional notes I envision exploring as our firm's design vision evolves. All are evident in the four projects presented here, which will be completed over the next two years.

TORONTO, ONTARIO

As a child, I visited friends in the Welsh countryside and was fascinated by the fact that they lived in a compound of separate buildings connected by walls or covered passageways: house, stable, sheds, and barn. It was a residence as a village, which is something that I've always loved. We revisited that idea when we were asked to create a house on 150 acres in the horse country near Toronto. Our concept is a series of six buildings, each one different in scale and linked by low flat-roof connectors and courtyards, some of them more private than others or visible only from one building or another. There are pools of water, too, emerging from low arches, some of them open, others enclosed by grilles. The arrangement reminds me a bit, in a vastly less structured way, of the multiple structures that make up the historic Fairmount Water Works in Philadelphia, only on a domestic scale.

Sheathed in shingles, our buildings sit on bases of local fieldstone that are slightly canted inwards, a gesture that emphasizes how they bear the weight of the structures above. Sharp angles and turns become overhangs or covering for porches, and visors and dormers appear to have been sliced out and pulled out or upwards. Some are interior, some are exterior, some are glazed, and others are solid, depending on what sort of view is being emphasized; others are just stone walls. As a result, the compound has an episodic quality, offering different moods and change of scale as you make your way from one element to another. The experience is like walking through a village.

After traveling about a mile down the drive, you reach a square walled courtyard. There, you ascend a flight of steps and pass through an arch that leads to the two-story entrance hall, its center a tile-lined conical form that is thirty-five-feet high and streaked with sunlight, thanks to a rooftop clerestory. From there, a corridor that is stone on one side and glazed on the other—offering a courtyard view—leads to the main part of the house. The windows of the house are restricted to the opposite side of the building, overlooking the pastures. A glass-enclosed spiraling staircase does the same. The initial glazed corridor also branches off to another pavilion that is dedicated to the main suite and dressing rooms. There is also a pool house and a garage in the sequence of joined structures. Only the barn is not part of the overall composition, being a working agricultural building. It is linked visually while maintaining a comfortable distance.

One of the early conceptual sketches shows a radiant placement of buildings around a long swimming pool.

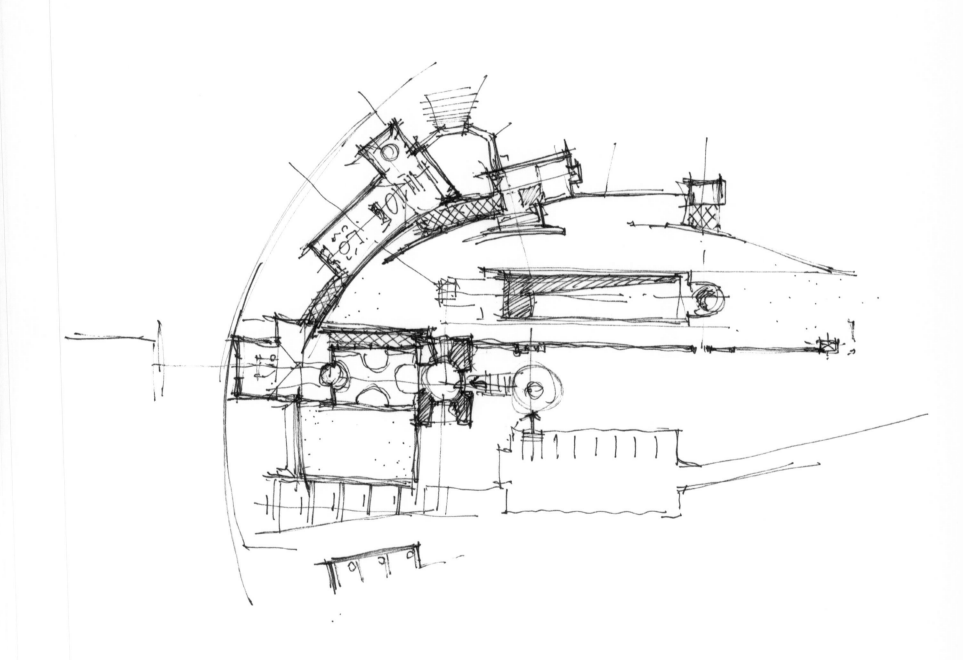

ABOVE AND OPPOSITE: *Rough-hewn local stone adds both texture and color to the walls.* **OVERLEAF:** *Rendering of the garden elevation, which incorporates gables and overhangs of the shingle style on a crisp fieldstone plinth.*

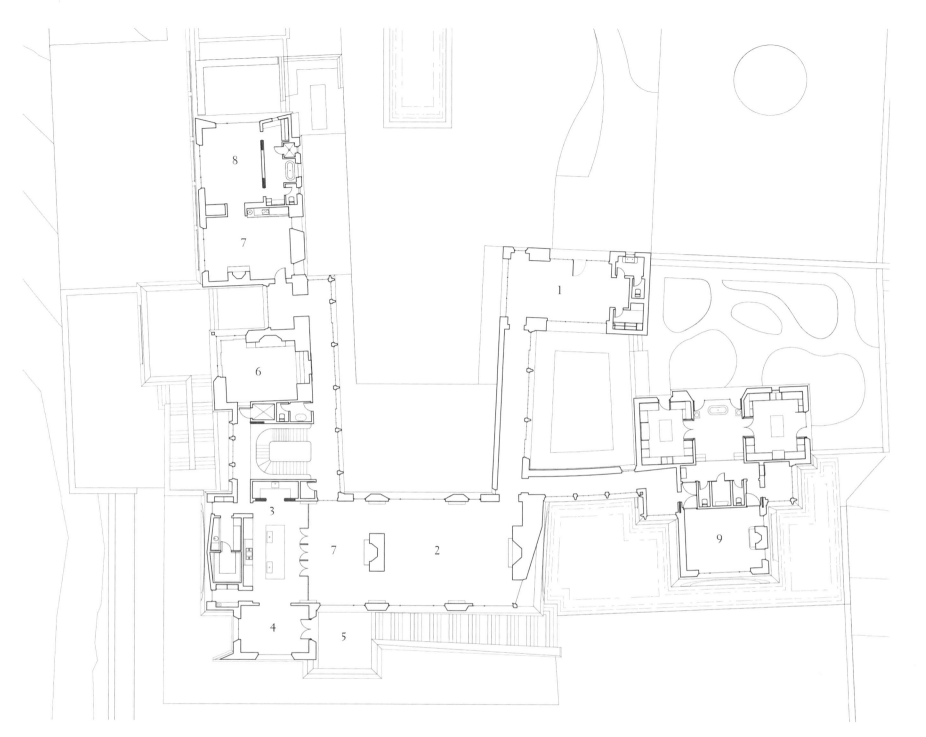

FIRST FLOOR PLAN

ENTRANCE ELEVATION

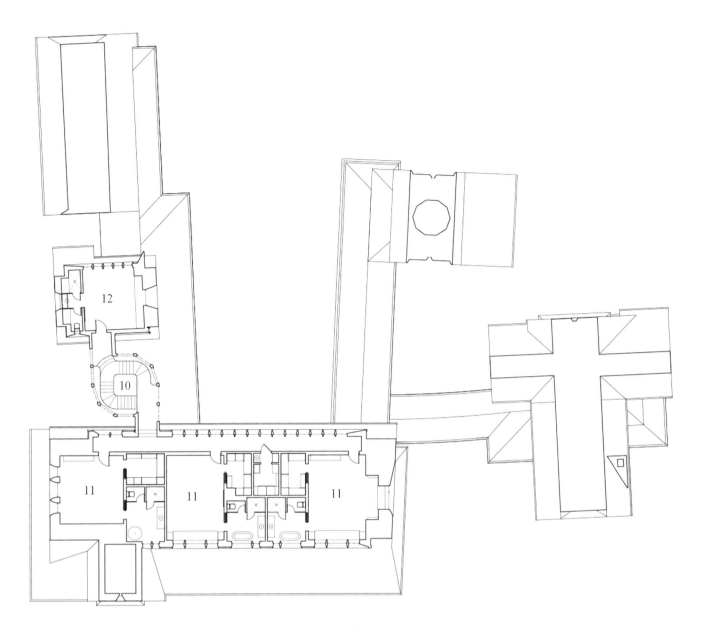

SECOND FLOOR PLAN

N   0   10   20   40   80

first floor

1. Entry
2. Living/Dining
3. Kitchen
4. Breakfast room
5. Terrace
6. Family room
7. Sitting room
8. Guest room
9. Primary suite

second floor

10. Stair hall
11. Guest room
12. Study

SOUTHAMPTON, NEW YORK

Here, on a narrow, ocean-front lot, the front door has been placed at the east side of the house—up an open stone stairway set within trees and native plants. I like buildings that make me try to find the entrance, that make me search for a point of entry; it is a quest that offers a different kind of experience from just opening the front door, walking into a central hall, and out the back. Here, the bronze door opens to an enfilade that spans the entire length of the house, all the way to a window at the west end. You haven't seen the ocean view yet but that does not matter—the enfilade and its 13-foot ceilings are impressive in a different way, thanks to varying amounts of light. There is a relatively dark entrance hall, a brilliantly lit stair hall, a bit of darkness again, then more light, and so on, all the way to that far window. That modulation of space and light offers sensuality as well as mystery and surprise. As you navigate your way forward, suddenly, on the left, you come across an open porch that frames the terrace and the ocean beyond.

The house is essentially symmetrical and axial, an I-shape structure with two pedimented pavilions joined by a stretch of bedrooms on the land front and stacked porches on the ocean side, the upper one being screened and the lower one open and shaded by a minimalist, cantilevered awning. The base of the house is Chinese granite, and Jerusalem stone clads the upper levels, while above, the pediments and roof are shingled. Jerusalem stone is a dense, durable material that holds up to saltwater; its warm beige tone also complements the weathered wood elements, including the unfinished teak windows, which will eventually turn gray like the shingles. The house will become largely monochrome as it ages. It was important, though, to emphasize the materiality of the random-course limestone

blocks, to give the stone more dimensionality. We distressed the surface by mimicking an old technique called shot sawn, where irregular lines were scratched across the stone with wire and steel shot, carving it in a way that suggests natural erosion. The diamond-shaped chimneys are composed of the same limestone, but it has been cut into long slender elements in the manner of ancient Roman brick, sixteen inches long by one-and-one-half inches thick. The stacked texture contrasts with the big blocks of limestone used elsewhere, while the smaller segments used for the chimneys echo the roof shingles around them.

When a building is orthogonal but combined with diagonal elements like the diamond chimneys and the chamfered limestone that frames the windows, the whole structure becomes more of a sculpture and less of a box. Blade-like stone columns—a shape inspired by projections at Lutyens's Castle Drogo in Devon, England—march around the exterior of the family room at the west end of the main facade. Additional blades, stretching from the foundation to the roofline, delineate the terminating pavilions on the oceanside elevation, like sections of wall that have been folded out from the main structure. Like the chimneys, they break up the right-angle form of the house and give it more plasticity; the center blades almost disappear while the end blades are splayed outward. As a result, as you make your way across the lawn and look at the house from different angles, the blades seem to subtly move, as if they are opening and closing.

Shadows and sunlight affect the blades, too, just as they interact with the myriad textures of the materials, from the overlapping shingles to the shot-sawn limestone. As our firm's designs increasingly bear witness, this is a house that is intended to offer new visual experiences every minute of the day.

OPPOSITE: *Sketch studying the movement of the blades.* OVERLEAF: *Rendering of the garden elevation, with shingles juxtaposed with limestone blocks and slender stone "bricks" on the chimneys.*

OPPOSITE: *Skylit porch to the second-floor office.* ABOVE: *Shingles will weather differently, depending on their position, adding color and texture to the surface.*

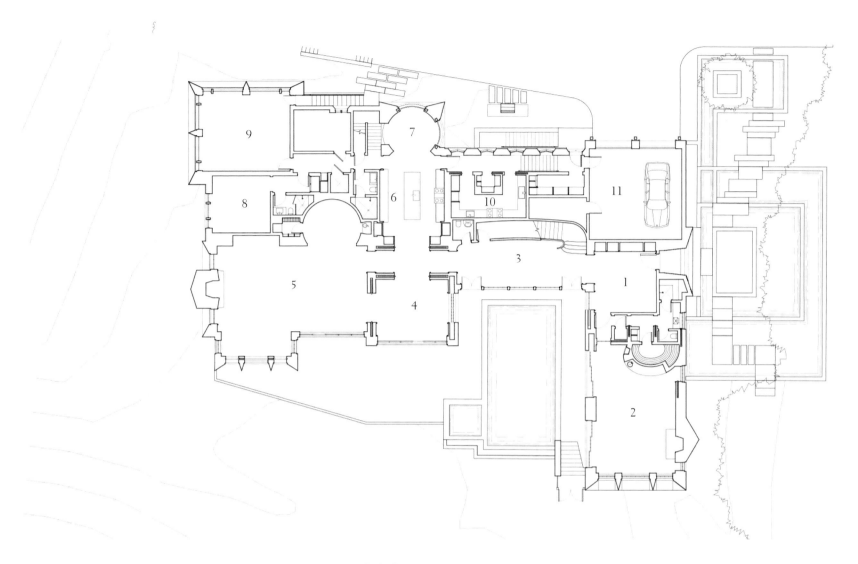

FIRST FLOOR PLAN

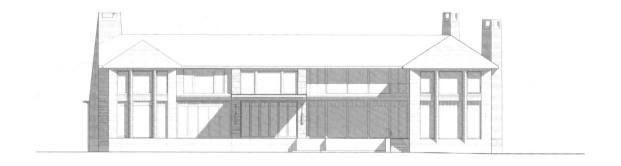

GARDEN ELEVATION

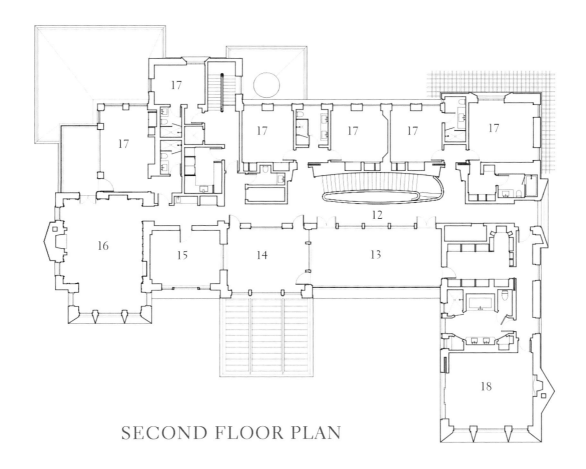

SECOND FLOOR PLAN

N

0   10   20   40   80

first floor

1. Entry
2. Screened porch
3. Stair hall
4. Dining room
5. Living room
6. Kitchen
7. Breakfast room
8. Guest room
9. Gym
10. Service kitchen
11. Garage

second floor

12. Stair hall
13. Covered porch
14. Screened porch
15. Study
16. Family room
17. Guest room
18. Primary suite

DALLAS, TEXAS

This design is a culmination of ideas we have been considering for the past ten years. The clients spend a portion of their year on Cape Cod and love shingle style architecture, which is not a typical Texas idiom. Drawing on the Southern penchant for white-painted brick, in this house we blended the two vocabularies so that one emerges from the other, a bit of New England rising from a masonry cradle. We bent and twisted the planes so the house seems to have been folded rather than constructed, from the beak-like hood with the central crease that shelters the discreet off-center entrance to the overhangs that seem to emerge from the roofline and have been tilted into place. Windows with deeply chamfered edges punctuate the facades, their depth adding another sense of their having been shaped, as if they have been carved out of the building with a chisel. From curved ceilings to chamfered windows, doorways, and fireplace niches, the interior spaces suggest the act of carving as well, as if the building started out as a block of stone and was gradually transformed into a living space.

From the back of the house, the primary blade chimney gives the impression of a mainsail, while it and the other two chimneys—you could think of them as headsails—appear to be cutting through the house in another dynamic gesture. That's echoed in the chamfered brick piers that are coplanar with the whole facade as well as the veranda's triangular columns. The verticality of the chimneys and the roofline is anchored by horizontal elements: parallel rows of shingles and painted brick, muntins reminiscent of Frank Lloyd Wright, louvers that frame the pool house, roofs that stretch out, the steps that terrace the landscape. The Dallas landscape is flat, and I wanted the building to reflect, but not be bound by it; the house hugs the ground as it soars.

Here, more than in any of my houses to date, the plan incorporates a series of curves. Gentle arcs define the public spaces, from sweeping galleries to the subtly torqued library and living room. Several of the major rooms, the dining room among them, are circular. Yet these forms are always anchored by a solidity and strength that keeps the house from feeling unbalanced or experimental. Logic and balance are always our guides in every aspect of the house, from initial gesture to smallest detail.

The covered porch overlooking the garden is gently curved.

RIGHT: *Sketch of the entrance facade, where an asymmetrical gable culminates in a towering chimney.* OVERLEAF: *Rendering of the garden facade, where a curved porch spans the ends of the house.*

Renderings of the circular dining room with an oculus reminiscent of the work of Texan James Turrell and the entrance hall.

HOUSTON, TEXAS

For this family house we have incorporated a significant amount of brick, but we have arranged it in shapes—such as the sawtooth motifs that trim the gables, with the brick ends perpendicular to the roof bond patterns. As a result, the walls will appear to be woven or even embroidered. The texture has a needlepoint quality, especially as sunlight skims across the surface variations.

Evoking the traditional Southern leitmotif of whitewashed brick, the exterior walls will be coated in a slurry of off-white mortar that resembles a huge piece of chalk. The stone lintels and caps are the same color as the slurry, and the wood porches—the only non-masonry elements on the exterior—will weather to a similar tone.

This is a muscular building, with a sense of permanence, of mass, one that is built for the ages. At their thinnest, the walls are about three feet thick, and at their thickest, such as the recess around the front door, they are as much as seven feet. It is a solid house broken up with transparency; you can see straight through it in places. The plan is as tightly knit as the brick patterns. Everything is on a centerline: every axis is met by a doorway or a gable or a centered window or a staircase. The gardens and courtyards are organized to extend this interwoven plan outside, with hedges, allées, water features, orchards, and lawns.

My favorite Lutyens country house is Marshcourt, in Hampshire, England, and there are certainly echoes of it here, from the off-white exterior (which at Marshcourt is clunch, a chalky lime-stone) to the largely timber interiors. Our project is a masonry box constructed around a frame of silvery gray wood. Our goal is to play with the surfaces, creating movement and action out of static materials. Here, the steel-framed windows are set within chamfered openings. Arches are elliptical. Gable ends are plumb, their sides are canted, the walls up to the eaves very gently tilt in. The chimneys are flared polygons with chamfered vents, and the side of the chimneys that face the roof ridges are beveled.

The building may be broad-shouldered, even brawny, at first glance, but there is a great deal of subtlety as well as variety, both present and future. As time goes by, sections of slurry gently slough off, revealing pinkish brick beneath, giving the house a homey softness under the Texas live oaks.

OPPOSITE: Rendering of the living hall from the dining room—a layering of soft, weathered oak timber. OVERLEAF: Rendering of the entrance elevation facing formal plantings of boxwood and an allée of linden trees.

Rendering of an outdoor fireplace under the brick vaulted porch. Steel windows and doors are delicately inserted into the masonry openings.

271

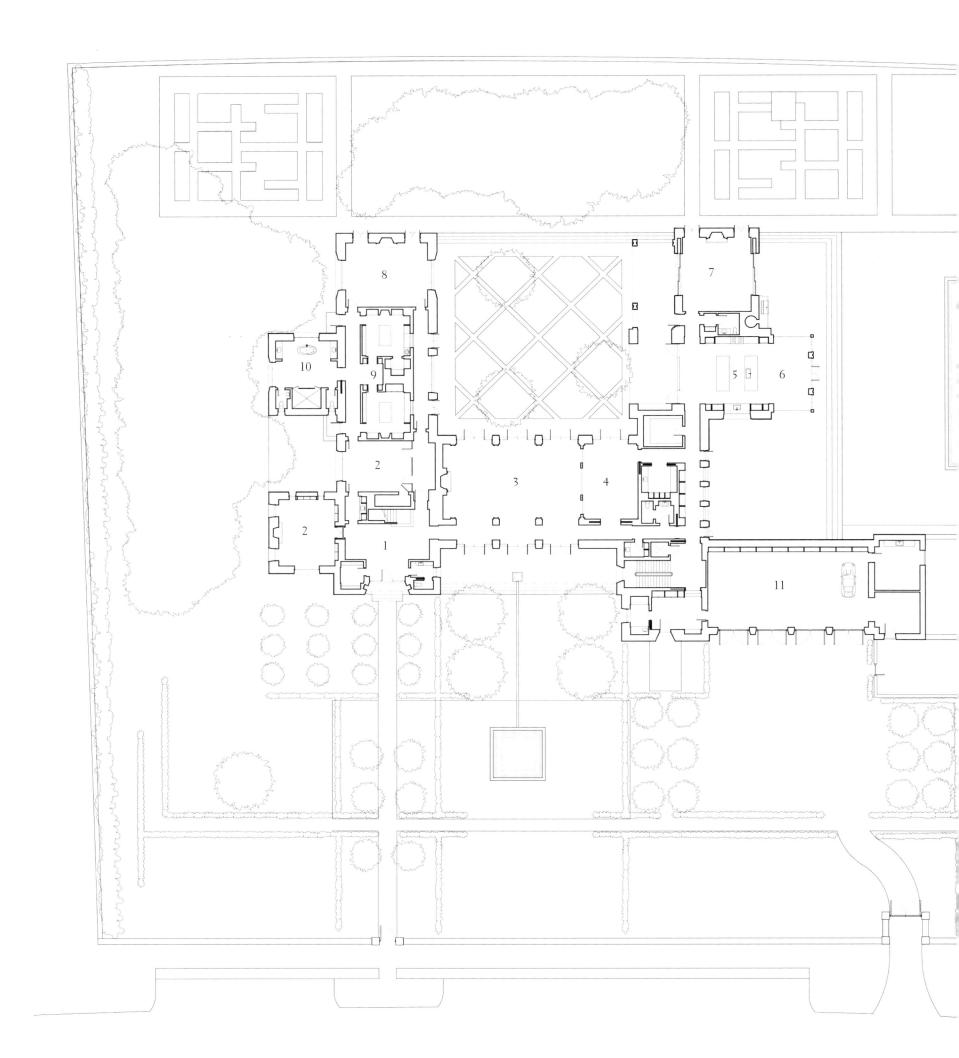

FIRST FLOOR PLAN

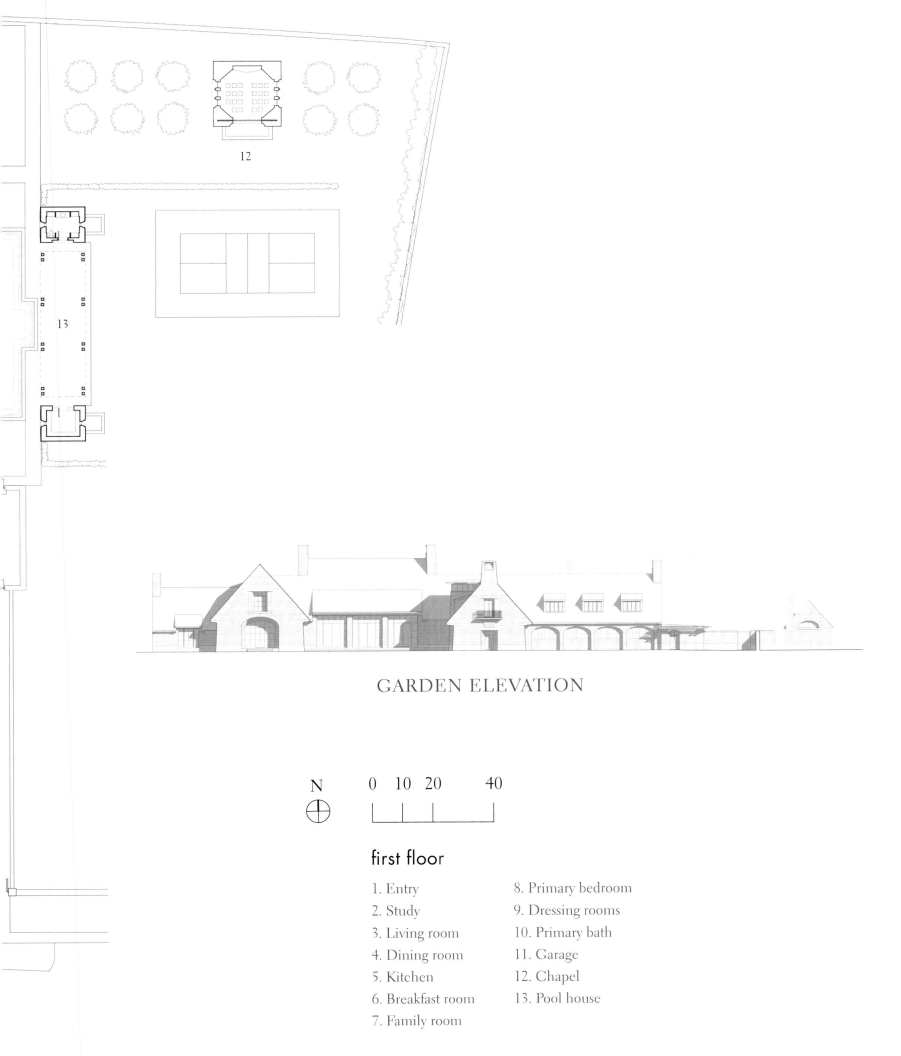

GARDEN ELEVATION

N ⊕

0 10 20 40

first floor

1. Entry
2. Study
3. Living room
4. Dining room
5. Kitchen
6. Breakfast room
7. Family room
8. Primary bedroom
9. Dressing rooms
10. Primary bath
11. Garage
12. Chapel
13. Pool house

PROJECT CREDITS

UPPER BROOKVILLE, NEW YORK

Architect: John Toya
Builder: Al Gherlone, Qualico Contracting Corporation
Landscape design: Steven R. Krog, Steven R. Krog Landscape PC
Interior design: Bruce Van Hoover, Simon Van Hoover Associates, Inc.
Photography: Peter Aaron, OTTO

LAKE KEOWEE, SOUTH CAROLINA

Architect: Winnie Yen*
Project staff: Alexander B. Colucci*
Builder: Malcolm Morgan and Brian Greene, Morgan-Keefe Builders, Inc.
Landscape design: Barry Cosgrove, Barry Cosgrove Landscaping, Inc.
Interior design: William Peace, Peace Design
Photography: Richard Powers

MARTHA'S VINEYARD, MASSACHUSETTS

Architect: Alexander Eng**
Project staff: Courtney Rombough, Hans Herrmann
Builder: John G. Early, John G. Early Contractor & Builder, Inc.
Interior design Terri Ricci, Mia Jung, Elizabeth Sesser, Ike Kligerman Barkley
Photography: Peter Aaron, OTTO

WATER MILL, NEW YORK

Architects: Jessica Wilks*, Andrew Dolan*
Builder: Don McAulay and Vincent C. Galardi, Seascape Partners
Landscape design: Ed Hollander, Melissa Reavis, Hollander Design Landscape Architects
Interior design: Victoria Hagen, Victoria Hagen Interiors
Photography: Richard Powers

SAGAPONACK, NEW YORK

Architect: Zephyr Fang*
Builder: Bill Costello, Michael Guyer, Men at Work Construction
Landscape design: Ed Hollander, Hollander Design Landscape Architects
Interior design: Ellie Cullman, Alyssa Urban, Katie Sutton, Cullman & Kravis Associates
Photography: Eric Piasecki and William Waldron (p. 124)

EAST HAMPTON, NEW YORK

Architects: Zephyr Fang*, Jessica Wilks*
Builder: Bill Costello, Bob Viola, Men at Work Construction
Landscape design: Ed Hollander, Melissa Reavis, Hollander Design Landscape Architects
Interior design: Francis D'Haene, D'Apostrophe Design, Inc.
Photography: Richard Powers

SEATTLE, WASHINGTON

Architect: Joe Carline**
Builder: Jim Dow, Dowbuilt
Landscape design: Dodi Fredericks, Fredericks Landscape Architecture
Interior design: Mia Jung, Elizabeth Sesser, Patricia Cassidy, Ike Kligerman Barkley
Photography: Richard Powers

WATCH HILL, RHODE ISLAND

Architects: Alexander Eng**, Drew Davis**, Joe Carline**, Zephyr Fang*
Project staff: Seung Park
Builder: Dennis R. Clarke, Dennis R. Clarke Contractor
Landscape design: Worcester + Worcester Landscape Architects
Interior design: Heather Wells, Heather Wells, Inc.
Photography: William Waldron and Nick Ventura (p. 206–207)

BRIDGEHAMPTON, NEW YORK

Architects: Jessica Wilks*, Andrew Dolan*
Builder: Ed Bulgin and Bill Pawlowski, Bulgin + Associates
Landscape design: Ed Hollander, Melissa Reavis, Hollander Design
Landscape Architects
Interior design: Timothy Haynes and Kevin Roberts, Haynes-Roberts, Inc.
Photography: Richard Powers

TORONTO, CANADA

Architects: Jessica Wilks*, Alexander B. Colucci*, Zephyr Fang*
Project staff: Stefani Santeramo
Builder: Tysen Lee, WPML, Inc.
Landscape design: Fernando Martos, Mariyam Villar Lopez, Fernando
Martos Landscape Design
Interior design: Kelly Wearstler, Luke Kielion, Kelly Wearstler
Renderings: Hayes Davidson, London

SOUTHAMPTON, NEW YORK

Architects: Drew Davis**, Winnie Yen*
Project Staff: Zephyr Fang, Ilana Simhon, Andrew Kim
Builder: George Gavalas, BUILDTHEORY
Landscape design: Ed Hollander, Melissa Reavis, Hollander Design
Landscape Architects
Interior design: Nikki Rosenthal, Bespoke Interior Design
Renderings: Hayes Davidson, London

DALLAS, TEXAS

Architects: Margie Lavender**, Andrew Dolan*
Project staff: Eric Manahan, Josh Melton
Builder: John Sebastian, Sebastian
Landscape design: David Hocker, Hocker Design Group
Interior design: Shelby Wagner, Shelby Wagner Design
Renderings: Hayes Davidson, London

HOUSTON, TEXAS

Architect: Drew Davis**
Project staff: Ilana Simhon, Kyle Ramey, Josh Melton, Betsy Shuttleworth
Builder: John Sebastian, Sebastian
Landscape design: Arne Maynard, Giulia Puccini, Arne Maynard
Garden Design
Interior design: Michael Misczynski, Atelier AM
Renderings: Hayes Davidson, London

**principal
*associate

ACKNOWLEDGMENTS

Designing a new house starts with a quick sketch. Little by little, the building develops and, with more accurate drawing and testing of ideas, it moves to reality as construction is done and the owners move in. I have never counted the number of people who work on a house, but directly and indirectly, it must be hundreds. On a smaller scale, a book follows a similar process—many are involved, and I am grateful to all of them.

Thank you to my extraordinary clients. These houses exist because of you, and I am grateful for your trust. And to the talented builders, craftspeople, and artisans who make drawings into beautiful buildings. Likewise, the many consultants, from waterproofing to lighting, who make building possible, thank you. To my colleagues in the design profession, interior designers, landscape architects, and fellow architects: I am grateful for the push and pull among us that makes the work stronger.

Thank you, Nancy Greystone, with whom many conversations led to the formation of the ideas expressed explicitly or implicitly in this book.

Andrew Dolan led the charge on the digital renderings and drawings between finding time to make a number of the houses in this volume even better. Eric Manahan spent hours bringing polish to the photographs and drawings. To Mississippi State University interns Luke Murray and Travis Bryan, thank you for the painstaking drawing of the sites, floor plans, and elevations.

Nothing happens without the counsel of Sara Frantz whose steady nature, kind but firm advice, masterful organizational skills, and clear-eyed judgment I rely on every day. This book, and the success of the practice for that matter, could not happen without her.

Thank you to the photographers, especially Richard Powers for the documentation of the work in a brilliant, evocative, and masterful way. And for the earlier projects, thank you to Peter Aaron, Eric Piasecki, Nick Ventura, and William Waldron. Your images capture the grand gesture as well as the finest detail of the work, allowing readers to experience these homes viscerally and with wonder. And to Anita Sarsidi, who manages to always show our work to its best advantage.

The writing was born of many conversations with Mitchell Owens—thank you for capturing and making the voice of these buildings sing. After years of reading your writing, it has been an honor to work with you.

Yolanda Cuomo, thank you for your incredible eye and the style and drama you bring to the printed page. With Bobbie Richardson, you have brought these houses to life in a new way.

Elizabeth White has, once again with great grace and insight, guided this architecture book through the creative process. I have a few more in me—I hope you do, as well.

Thank you, Cynthia Conigliaro, dear friend since college, who over thirty years has helped build my architectural library from her beloved Archivia Books, for shepherding this book from idea to reality. This book is richer and more beautiful for your experience, intuition, and knowledge.

Thank you, always, to my daughters, Magdalen, Katherine, and Rebecca, and my wife, Kristin, who make it all worthwhile.

First published in the United States by The Monacelli Press.
All rights reserved.

Library of Congress Control Number: 2022934361
ISBN: 9781580936040

YOLANDA CUOMO DESIGN
Associate Designer: Bobbie Richardson

Printed in Italy

Monacelli
A Phaidon Company
65 Bleecker Street
New York, New York 10012